D1625100

CHRIST,
MY
COMPANION

CHRIST, MY COMPANION

MEDITATIONS ON THE PRAYER OF ST. PATRICK

MARILYN CHANDLER MCENTYRE

BakerBooks

a division of Baker Publishing Group
Grand Rapids, Michigan

© 2008 by Marilyn Chandler McEntyre

Published by Baker Books
a division of Baker Publishing Group
P.O. Box 6287, Grand Rapids, MI 49516-6287

Printed in the United States of America

All rights reserved. No part of this publication may be reproduced, stored in a retrieval system, or transmitted in any form or by any means—for example, electronic, photocopy, recording—without the prior written permission of the publisher. The only exception is brief quotations in printed reviews.

ISBN-13: 978-0-7394-9855-2

Unless otherwise indicated, Scripture is taken from the HOLY BIBLE, NEW INTER-NATIONAL VERSION®. NIV®. Copyright © 1973, 1978, 1984 by International Bible Society. Used by permission of Zondervan. All rights reserved.

Scripture marked ESV is taken from The Holy Bible, English Standard Version, copyright © 2001 by Crossway Bibles, a division of Good News Publishers. Used by permission. All rights reserved.

Scripture marked KJV is taken from the King James Version of the Bible.

For Henry, whose singing of this hymn has blessed me,
and for John, who has helped me understand it
in the concrete particulars of daily living,
with love and thanks

CONTENTS

ACKNOWLEDGMENTS

I wish to thank Ruth Cheadle for her patient and encouraging assistance, my husband, John, for patient listening and thoughtful reading, and our children for the inspiration they bring and the gifts they are.

Christ be with me,
Christ within me,
Christ behind me,
Christ before me,
Christ beside me,
Christ to win me,
Christ to comfort and restore me.
Christ beneath me,
Christ above me,
Christ in quiet,
Christ in danger,
Christ in hearts of all that love me,
Christ in mouth of friend and stranger.

From an adaptation of a section of
"St. Patrick's Breastplate" by Cecil Alexander and
Charles Stanford. Original prayer attributed to
St. Patrick, early fifth century

INTRODUCTION

Those of us whose Sunday worship includes a recitation of the Nicene Creed reaffirm weekly that we believe in the communion of saints. I have come to appreciate this article of faith more as life has led me to some of those saints, to be taught by their examples, their writings, and the prayers they have left behind for those of us still finding our way in a world still fallen, still hopeful.

The prayer widely known as "St. Patrick's Breastplate," attributed to St. Patrick, fifth-century missionary to Ireland, offers a rich range of reflection on scriptural teaching, Christian theology, and the mystery of Christ's presence. The first stanzas of that prayer begin with the repeated phrase "I bind unto myself today" as though with each declaration of the articles of faith he girded himself for encounters with the often hostile pagans among whom he ventured to bring the gospel story. The utterance of the truths he believed seemed to carry an almost sacramental power for him. His enumeration of these truths invites us, line by line, to contemplate the breadth and height and depth of Christ's power and love.

The popular Anglican hymn that goes by the same name as the original prayer, and provides the focus of these reflections, was adapted by Cecil Alexander in 1889 and set to music by Charles Stanford in 1902. Its lyrics represent relatively small sections of the much longer original prayer but retain much of the power of the whole to invite meditation and renew a sense of the mystery and magnitude of the one who was called Emmanuel— God with us.

My own reflections on each of the lines in the refrain of that hymn have enabled me to see how easy it is to fall into habits of mind that limit our sense of the holy and of God's presence, of who Christ is, and of how the Spirit moves among us. Each of the prepositions in the prayer opens a new avenue of awareness. Humble parts of speech that they are, they offer helpful reminders of God's many ways of being made manifest.

In the course of writing about this prayer, I had to come to terms with my own ways of understanding and imagining the presence of Christ, who promises to be with us always. In places I move rather freely among the persons of the Trinity, assuming that most who read these pages will accept all three persons as dimensions of the Holy One who has no gender, who, though revealed in Scripture, is beyond our imagining, and whose name is a verb: I AM. I want to acknowledge the seriousness and value of the contemporary conversation taking place in the church about how to reference the persons of the Trinity, and about the problematic character of the patriarchy from which that language emerges. After wrestling with that question I decided, because the text under consideration is an ancient prayer and the person upon whom that prayer is focused is specifically Jesus, the Christ, to use the male pronoun throughout to refer to the persons of the Trinity. It is not an entirely comfortable decision, but I believe the alternatives (or alternation among them) would be distracting. I hope that decision will not make these reflections less inviting or in any way diminish appreciation of the prayer that occasioned them.

St. Patrick "bound unto himself" the truths he knew and claimed in order to equip himself for work in a pagan world. In a world where not only faith but also the precious truth-bearing instrument of language itself are so often oversimplified, flattened into cliché, and turned to unworthy purposes, a prayer like this offers a model for faithful, systematic reclamation. It is my hope that these reflections will give readers an incentive to revisit the original prayer in its entirety, to dwell among its lovely lines, and to enjoy the spiritual refreshment they provide.

There is more to plumb than prepositions in St. Patrick's beautiful prayer. But together, this litany of prepositions reminds us of the breadth of an embrace so encompassing that we are never outside it. Held safe in life and in death by the God whose "center is everywhere and whose periphery is nowhere,"[1] who is within, beside, behind, before, below, and above, we can lie down in peace, abiding in him as he abides in us, knowing, like the psalmist, that even if we "take the wings of the morning and dwell in the uttermost parts of the sea" (Ps. 139:9 ESV), even there we will be met and greeted and loved.

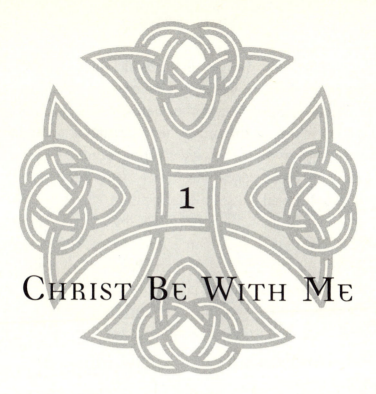

CHRIST BE WITH ME

O ne of the most comforting promises in the Gospels is Jesus' assurance "Behold, I am with you always, even unto the end of the age" (Matt. 28:20). "Listen," might be another translation. Be assured of this. Don't forget this. I AM with you. Always. Wherever you are.

One of our deepest human needs is not to be alone. Even those of us who cherish solitude do not want to be isolated or abandoned. We can all remember the dark nights or sick days when the thing we wanted most was a parent at the bedside who promised to stay by us while we slept. To fall asleep in the presence of a loving, watchful gaze is to relax into a place of healing. A great benefit of marital companionship is the shared silences—reading together in the same room, exchanging a remark now and then, happy in simply being with one another. All the love songs that croon "I will never leave you" lie. But Jesus' promise fully addresses the longing those songs evoke. He will abide with us. We will not be abandoned. Though not always in the ways we imagine or want, he will show up, hang around, and, as Eugene Peterson translates it, "pitch his tent" among us and be our neighbor.

The scriptural blessing "the Lord be with you," repeated daily and weekly in liturgies throughout the world, contains and imparts more than a gesture of goodwill. It is a summoning, a reminder, an assurance, an act of solidarity. In Chronicles, it is followed by the very practical addendum "so that you may succeed in building the house of the LORD your God" (1 Chron. 22:11 ESV). The Lord comes to be with us, in response to our call, to aid in his assigned purposes. In coming, he provides the energy, the will, the resources. A few verses later, the blessing is repeated, almost as an imperative: "Arise and work! The Lord be with you!" (I am reminded of the curious, lively use of the subjunctive in certain African-American dialects that move "be" from its decorous place in the seldom-used subjunctive mode into the bold foreground

16

of the indicative. "He be here!" somehow resounds with conviction greater than the simple declaration "He is here.") He *is* here, as Jeremiah reminds us, to "deliver" us (Jer. 1:19 ESV), to "save" us (Jer. 30:11 ESV), to "deal with" us (Ezek. 20:44 ESV). The writer of Chronicles reiterates God's promise as a rhetorical question, insisting that his hearers consider the evidence and be satisfied: "Is not the LORD your God with you?" he asks. "And has he not given you peace on every side?" (1 Chron. 22:18 ESV). We know that God is with us when peace reigns, and when God is with us, our knowing is certain.

One sure sign that Christ is with me is that I am not subject to debilitating fear. Courage, like peace, is a sign of Christ's presence. At least, perhaps, we can say that when we become aware of and confident in that presence, fear begins to evaporate. "Even though I walk through the valley of the shadow of death, I will fear no evil, for you are with me," the psalmist writes (Ps. 23:4). These words, read at generations of deathbeds and to children going to sleep in the dark, are a powerful, simple declaration of trust. You are with me. And so I am completely safe. In life and in death. This understanding of safety, to be sure, requires a larger awareness of what we are about than the visible, material facts of this precarious world where airborne viruses and radioactive particles and speeding cars threaten our earthly lives on every side. But again and again, as the long story of salvation unfolds, the God who came to us in Christ and remains with us in Spirit reiterates this encouragement: "Fear not, for I am with you; be not dismayed, for I am your God; I will strengthen you, I will help you, I will uphold you" (Isa. 41:10 ESV). In the lion's den and in the midst of terrifying visions, Daniel received the same assurance when a heavenly being appeared to him: "'O man greatly loved, fear not, peace be with you; be strong and of good courage.' And as he spoke to me," the writer recalls, "I was strengthened" (Dan. 10:19 ESV).

Scripture is replete with images that broach the mystery of Christ's presence with us and among us, constant and instant and surprising and faithful. He is with us as the light that surrounds us—the medium in which we live and move and are embraced and guided. "God is light," John writes. "In him there is no darkness at all" (1 John 1:5). When we place ourselves in that divine light, we see things differently—perhaps, at times, the way Eugene Peterson suggested when he made the exuberant claim, "For eyes that can see, every bush is a burning bush." The God who is light, who unveiled Christ in the transfiguration, also blinded Paul on the road to Damascus. He is, as Emily Dickinson put it, the truth that "must dazzle gradually—or every man be blind."[1]

In the light of Christ, the things of this world are no longer ours, but God's, and we know all our privilege as gift and begin to live in gratitude. Gradually, we come to see that in this lively world "charged with the grandeur of God"[2] the things we have been conditioned to regard as nouns are actually verbs—living, growing, dying, regenerating, being transformed by the hand of a generous and endlessly bountiful Creator. Familiar landscapes become enlivened with a new dimensionality—infused and energized like Van Gogh's cypresses that leap and stretch, yearning to reach just beyond that edge where matter becomes energy. "With you," the psalmist writes, "is the fountain of life; in your light do we see light" (Ps. 36:9). Notice the shift of focus: the light of God's presence brings us into an awareness of fluidity, movement, the surging, pulsing character of life itself, and what we are used to seeing as objects may be seen more properly as manifestations of light itself—gatherings of energy into what we call matter, for a little time, until the wind blows over them and they are gone: gone from one plane of awareness, reconfigured in ways we cannot yet perceive.

The One who comes to us as light comes to us as peace. When we summon him, sudden, inexplicable, irrational peace descends on us even in the midst of trouble: practice the faith you have learned, Paul admonishes the Philippians, "and the God of peace will be with you" (Phil. 4:9 ESV). The mark of the presence of the Prince of Peace is, perhaps, that divine illogic: Christ's peace is "not as the world gives," but a peace we commonly call courage and easily mistake for human virtue. Christ's promise "Peace I give you, my peace I leave you" is given in the same farewell discourse that ends in the promise to be with us always: in that peace. In the confidence that cannot be mustered by reckoning the odds, but only received by bowing and saying yes. The martyrs whose stories have survived centuries of troubling Christian history are distinguished by the remarkable peace that came to them at the stake or on the gibbet or standing before their executioners. Even allowing for the exaggerations of devoted biographers, the evidence is awe inspiring: Christ has been with those who were faithful unto death, in the eye of the storm and in the heat of fires, accompanying them as once Shadrach, Meshach, and Abednego were accompanied, not always forestalling death, but dispelling all fear of it.

The things we fear, Jesus teaches, are the wrong things. "Do not fear those who kill the body, but cannot kill the soul," he tells his followers. "Rather fear him who can destroy both body and soul in hell" (Matt. 10:28 ESV).

He comes to us in our fear as our protector. "The LORD of hosts is with us; the God of Jacob is our fortress," the psalmist writes. "With God we shall do valiantly" (Ps. 46:7, 60:12 ESV). When we are not doing valiantly, when we find ourselves mired in the muddiness of human circumstance, we have the promise that he will protect us even from ourselves: "When he calls to me, I will answer him; I will be with him in trouble; I will rescue him" (Ps. 91:15 ESV). The doing valiantly comes later. All we have to do is seek him. "Seek good, and not evil," Amos says simply, "that you may live; and so the Lord, the God of hosts, will be with you, as you have said" (Amos 5:14 ESV).

So many stories testify to the reality of divine accompaniment. When Joseph's brothers sold him into Egypt, we read, "God was with him" (Acts 7:9 ESV). And when Paul faced rejection and persecution among the Macedonians, Christ assured him in a vision, "Do not be afraid, but go on speaking and do not be silent, for I am with you, and no one will attack you to harm you" (Acts 18:10 ESV). God's promises grow extravagant, we notice, if we keep looking. They range from the humane to the miraculous: "When you pass through the waters, I will be with you; and through the rivers, they shall not overwhelm you; when you walk through fire you shall not be burned, and the flame shall not consume you" (Isa. 43:2 ESV).

21

Asp and viper, Philistines with swords, hostile nations with missiles poised will not destroy us. Unless we are seeing in the light Christ provides, these promises begin to look rather fanciful. Christ's protection, like Christ's peace, has to be understood in terms that take us beyond craven longing for self-preservation. Nothing is more abundantly clear in this world than that we will not be able to avoid death, and some of us will die violently. But Christ's promise to be with us is a promise to see us even through that hard passage—loving us even unto our death as he loved us even unto his.

In love he comes to us as friend, elder, and companion. "You hold my right hand," the psalmist writes, invoking a memory of childhood when the safest place for the right hand to be—the one that might later hold a sword or curl into a fist for ready defense—is enclosed in another, bigger, more capable hand. He is with us as a watchful parent in the night, guarding us even when we are utterly unconscious of divine presence and protection. What lovely satisfaction we find in the simple line, "I awake, and I am still with you" (Ps. 139:18 ESV). He "dwells" with us—one of the loveliest words in Scripture to describe a God who makes his home among us.

He dwells with us in our daily lives and in our lives of common worship. "Behold, I stand at the door and knock. If anyone hears my voice and opens the door, I will come in to him and eat with him, and he with me" (Rev. 3:20 ESV). The image of eating, of course, goes to the heart of the eucharistic experience. In the Eucharist, Christ enters into us as intimately as is possible in the physical universe. In his life, he moved from inhabiting a human body to sharing food with others to becoming food, again to enter into the life of the body in radical, shocking fact.

We most generally think of "with" in spatial terms— next to, beside, in proximity to. But Christ is "with" us in much more mysterious ways, and, contemplating that mystery, we may come to a much wider understanding of what it is to be with Christ and even with each other. "For thus says the One who is high and lifted up, who inhabits eternity, whose name is Holy: 'I dwell in the high and holy place, and also with him who is of a contrite and lowly spirit, to revive the spirit of the lowly, and to revive the heart of the contrite'" (Isa. 57:15 ESV). Evidently there is no separation between the "high and holy place" where the Holy One dwells and the heart of the humble that offers itself as his host.

Twentieth-century physics has yielded some amazing, mind-bending insights about the intimate, reactive connections among particles separated, in spatial terms, by light years but reactive to one another as though they were swirling in the same atomic orbit. Apparently distance is no barrier to connection, even in the physical world at its smallest and subtlest level. And so the paradoxical truths that God is both immanent and transcendent, both "in heaven" and "on earth," beyond us and also with us, may be resolved by shedding the conceptual paradigms that keep us caught in Newtonian physics and limiting metaphors, and opening ourselves instead to the mystery of omnipresence.

But Christ is with us in ways that are also simple, accessible, and ordinary. "By day the Lord commands his steadfast love, and at night his song is with me, a prayer to the God of my life," the psalmist writes (Ps. 42:8 ESV). Song, like prayer, brings us into the Lord's presence. Elie Wiesel speaks about song as the center and heart of story.[3] One of the ways God is with us is in the undercurrent of melody that gives shape and rhythm to the very breath of life. The Spirit who prays within us prays, it seems, not only with "groanings too deep for words" (Rom. 8:26 ESV), but also with song, singing to the rhythm of our very heartbeats, praying within us even as we sleep, our bodies and souls instruments of that singing.

Of course there are stories about God with us that are not about being held and comforted but rather about being confronted. Jacob "strove with God" (Hos. 12:3 ESV), argued with him, bargained with him; Jonah (laughably) fled him. To ask that Christ be with us is to ask not only for protection and reassurance, or even guidance, but also for a kind of awareness and accountability that can keep us at the edge of our comfort zone and in a place of radical vulnerability. The curious question Jesus asked the afflicted, "Do you want to be healed?" might also come to us with a similar note of challenge: Do you want my companionship? Are you ready for it? Can you rise to it? Will you trust in it?

Happily, though, the commonest answer to the prayer that Christ be with me comes in the form of ordinary human fellowship. God's words of comfort and challenge come to us through other human beings—messengers of God, sometimes unaware themselves that that is what they are. Burning bushes and pillars of light are rare, but God is present wherever we look—if we have eyes to see.

We were made for community, called into community, and so, for most of us most of the time, with others is where we find the spiritual nourishment and healing we need. At the heart of the pastoral vocation is the work of "being with"—or as some put it, "the ministry of presence." It is no simple matter to carry out that ministry. "Being with" can be more challenging than doing for. The "to do" list is laid aside. It is sometimes hard to think of the right thing to say. Silence is awkward. One doesn't want to intrude. And a ministering presence is not always welcome where it may be needed.

But the Gospels give us good guidance as to how we are to be with one another. Jesus called his followers together for uncertain journeys; he ate with tax collectors and sinners; he partied with the rich and braved the elements with the poor; he withdrew into solitude and returned to strengthen and teach; he healed and preached, encouraged and admonished, prayed aloud and in silence, comforted and warned. With man, he told them, many things are impossible, but "with God all things are possible" (Matt. 19:26 ESV). Christ's companionship empowers us. He has invited us into an unequal partnership, entirely to our benefit. With him, with the perspective he offers, our categories shift, and we begin to live in a new awareness on new terms.

"As the father has sent me, even so I am sending you" (John 20:21 ESV), he finally said, having shown his followers how to enter into each other's lives as healers and teachers, witnesses and friends, love-bearers and light-bearers. Our work, like theirs, is to be with one another, to minister to "the least of these," to do justice, to love mercy, and to walk humbly with the God who humbled himself to walk with us.

2

CHRIST WITHIN ME

This is the body of Christ," the pastor says. "Feed on it in your hearts, with thanksgiving." And so, as George Herbert puts it in his beautiful poem "Love Bade Me Welcome," we are welcomed to the table where our food is God's own self, made word made flesh made bread and wine. The sacrament of the Lord's Supper is an act of radical intimacy unlike any other. In it we encounter an outward and visible sign of an astonishing fact: that God has found a way into our very bodies and beings, to unite with us, breath and bone, and dwell in us. "Eat my body and drink my blood" is surely one of the most scandalous utterances in the story of salvation, and one of the strongest testimonies to the extravagance of an infinite God who pours out his Spirit "without limit" on humankind and yet enters into our limited lives and bodies to transform them.

The idea that Christ lives "within" each of us, intimately, personally, working in hidden ways both through and in spite of personality and circumstance, coexists paradoxically with the theological claim that we are "in Christ." "In him we live, and move, and have our being" (Acts 17:28 KJV). Karl Barth points to the centrality of this phrase in *Church Dogmatics*, where, after a long reflection on the phrase "in Christ," he insists, "We are invited and challenged to understand ourselves from this and not from any other standpoint."[1] We stand before God clothed in the very glory of Christ, imbedded, immersed, even buried in Christ to be resurrected and made new creatures by dwelling in and taking our nourishment from the very source of life.

At the same time, God dwells in us. The "indwelling" of the Holy Spirit, the idea that each of us participates in living out the "Christ life," as Caryll Houselander put it, the very real way Christ enters into us in the physical act of eating and drinking the bread and wine of the

Lord's Supper, all testify to the mysterious fact that God enters and abides in each of us, making us "temple[s] of the Holy Spirit" (1 Cor. 6:19). God is my dwelling place, and I am God's dwelling place. The latter claim places a high value on my body, soul, and consciousness as a site of God's self-manifestation in this world, in this place and time. So the Lord's Supper brings us face to face with this almost imponderable truth: God lives both with us and *in* us.

Receiving Christ in this way makes me a "carrier"; odious as the comparison may be, it is something like being a carrier of a virus. I may or may not be aware of its presence or that I am communicating it to others. As a Christ-bearer, I carry a communicable (and possibly airborne!) agent of healing and life. I am a bearer of life-giving power, sometimes quite in spite of myself. I may be a ramshackle and ill-tended dwelling, but I am also empowered as a member of Christ's body to be a locus and agent of grace.

Women have a particular biological access to the idea of bearing Christ within us by the simple fact that our bodies are spaces designed to be occupied. We are aware of ourselves from puberty as potential "carriers." This is a place where a theology developed in patriarchal culture can be tempered and informed by female experience: to know that we can carry a live being within our very bodies is to be deeply aware that we are made to be participants in the God-work of creating and sustaining life. Indeed, at the heart of our theology are stories of women—Sarah, Rebekah, Rachel, Ruth, Mary—who carried the seed of nations, the rescuers of peoples, secrets of salvation, and, ultimately, God's very self, to be born as a vulnerable infant into a conflicted world. And all of us, men included, are Christ-bearers who bring forth into the world not only actual children but the works and ways of being that the Spirit chooses to make manifest in each of us.

The core truth in this line of St. Patrick's prayer is that our God is a God who enters into the created order and inhabits it—who does not simply act upon us from above or afar but dwells at the heart of things, in the hearts (and even the entrails, as the King James Version would have it) of the very folk who fail and forsake him. God spoke to Moses from within the burning bush (Exod. 3:2) and from within the cloud that had settled on Mt. Sinai (Exod. 24:16). He is within the river whose streams "make glad the City of God" (Psalm 46) and within the Jerusalem, ringed with fire, that appeared in Zephaniah's vision. God is within our lungs, as well as our hearts and minds; every breath drawn and released is a receiving and releasing of life that comes directly from the God who breathed life into our first parents. "As long as I have life within me," Job writes, "the breath of God in my nostrils, my lips will not speak wickedness, and my tongue will utter no deceit" (Job 27:3).

One way the Old Testament writers recognized God's presence was in God's words. In Hebrew tradition utterance was sacred because words were born of and borne on the breath of life, which was *ruach*, spirit. The Torah was to be read aloud, not silently, because reading was understood as a way of taking part in creation—uttering forth the word, *dabar*, which also means "thing." Words are made of the breath of life, coming forth from within us, who are given the divine gift of speech, a too-often under-recognized form of power, consequential and rich with life-giving potential. So when the psalmist writes, "Your law is within my heart" (Ps. 40), the claim is more than metaphor; it is an acknowledgment of one of the mysterious ways God dwells within us, informing our minds and wills, reflected again in Proverbs where the speaker admonishes his son to "keep my words and store up my commands within you" (Prov. 7:1). "An oracle is within my heart," he writes, knowing that the very source of wisdom is closer to him than his very self (Ps. 36:1).

The language that recognizes and gives us access to the indwelling God shifts somewhat in the New Testament.

31

There, the accent shifts from God as present in natural phenomena, in the law, and in the mouths of prophets to God as fully manifest in Christ, historically real and present to his disciples, and then in the Spirit, promised and sent at Pentecost. God's ways of being among us and also within us become, in these accounts, both more literal and more mysterious. The kingdom of God is within you, Jesus says, and though some translations render the phrase "among you," either assures us of the immediacy of community and communion with a God who is not distant but closer than we can imagine.

Jesus admonishes his followers to tend to the "light within them" and promises that streams of living water will flow from within them. Receiving and channeling the energy of Christ, they (and we) may become light sources and life sources. Paul identifies Christ as the one "who is able to do immeasurably more than all we ask or imagine, according to his power that is at work within us" (Eph. 3:20). And how reassuring that what is at work within us is not limited to our imagination or control, but only inhabits us when we are willing vessels, needing only our consent. Again and again Paul identifies the central mystery of the faith he proclaims and teaches as "Christ in you" (Col. 3:3).

Christ in us is the same presence Pharaoh recognized in Moses when he asked, "Can we find anyone like this man, one in whom is the spirit of God?" (Gen. 41:38), and the same who dwelt in Joshua, readying him for anointing, and in Job, who insisted, "The Spirit of God has made me; the breath of the Almighty gives me life" (Job. 33:4). He is the same as the one who inspired the psalmist's song, and who, breathing on the apostles, infused them with his own Spirit and, as he promised, supplied them with all they needed in times of trial, so even in their darkest moments they were "filled" with the Holy Spirit.

Such plenitude in that term—"filled"! No stinting, no holding back, but infused with energy, exuberance, clarity, boldness, joy, power, understanding. To be born of that Spirit is to receive a whole new lease on life itself—to see it in a whole new set of terms. As Paul puts it, "I no longer live, but Christ lives in me" (Gal. 2:20). Ego gives way to a widened, transformed consciousness, available to divine intentions and fueled by divine power. We know that we live in him and he in us, John writes, "because he has given us of his Spirit" (1 John 4:13).

Consider the language we use to describe what we commonly recognize in people of great spiritual maturity and depth: *radiant, lively, fully present, luminous, creative, grounded*, and even, sometimes, *holy*. All these words suggest abundance of energy, a flexible, fluid quality of

33

responsiveness, an openness to the call of the moment, a sufficiency that gives and receives without the kind of neediness we've come to call codependency. When we extend our full hospitality to the Christ within us, we have all we need. The rest of what comes our way is pure gift, to be received with thanksgiving but without fear of loss or jealousy of possession.

So St. Patrick's prayer both reminds and invites us to turn our attention and bring our intentions to the Christ within us: Christ, who renews my life with every breath, who offers me direction when I quiet my mind, who empowers me to act despite my misgivings, who teaches me in dreams and in the sudden gifts of imagination, who prompts and urges, admonishes and clarifies, welcomes and comforts, fills up the dark corners with the light that casts out every darkness.

To focus on Christ, and on the God who has made us temples of the indwelling Spirit, is to practice the prayer of listening. Though not every impulse is divine guidance (by a long shot), and not every inner voice is God's, "within" is where we may find what we most need, away from the clatter and buzz of the marketplace and the media, away even from the many words that can drown out the still, small voice of the Spirit who speaks to those who have ears to hear. Much of the best prayer happens in waiting and listening. What comes in those times of prayer will have an element of precision and surprise one cannot quite reach if one fills the prayer space and prayer time with the busyness of thought. Mother Teresa's oft-cited answer to a reporter when he asked her what she said to God in prayer was "I listen." When he then asked, "What does God say?" she answered, "He listens."[2] The deep place beyond words that can only be reached in the self-abandonment of contemplative prayer requires a retreat from the teeming demands of the daily world into a sacred inner space, silent and open, where awareness of God's presence enters a new dimension.

One of the German words I like best is *hineinlauschen*—to listen into. I imagine listening like this as leaning into the conversation, the body eager and the mind open, without urgency to deliver one's own message, attentive not only to the words spoken, but to their possibilities, and to the silences between them. *Hineinlauschen* is a way of praying, and an attitude toward God that takes particular account of the Christ within as one to be listened for and listened to with every fiber of our being. When we pray like this we open space to be filled, and we are filled. We make ourselves hospitable, and we are inhabited.

When I am aware of the Christ within me, I become more aware of the Christ within you. An old Quaker saying, "There is that of God in everyone," echoes a wisdom not exclusive to Christian faith—that when we see one another rightly, we get a glimpse of God. We learn, perhaps slowly, to see each other in terms of the light shining through our various shadows and drawn shades. We learn to listen to each other as messengers and, if we are well practiced, like St. Benedict, to "receive all guests as Christ." Within us and among us, the long conversation of the Trinity, the speaking and answering of God to God, sounds new echoes and moves into a new key for new occasions. And so when the Christ in me recognizes and sings with the Christ in you, we act as the best selves we were called to be—members of the body of Christ. "In him," Paul writes, "you . . . are being built together to become a dwelling in which God lives by his Spirit" (Eph. 2:22). The Christ who is within me is the Christ who is among us. The kingdom of God is within you. The kingdom of God is among you. They are the same truth. The incarnation keeps unfolding. The Christ within me is a God who once again has placed God's very self in the precarious care of a human being, to be brought forth, attended to, and ushered into a world still waiting.

3

CHRIST BEHIND ME

My husband worked for Summit Expedition in its earliest years. Summit Expedition was a Christian organization that took young people on three-week treks in the Sierra wilderness to stretch their bodies and spirits. The position he fell into, that fit his particular pastoral temperament, was that of the hiker who brings up the rear, encourages the weary, motivates laggers, and attends to those who fall behind for any reason. The leader of the day forged on out in front, setting the pace and assessing upcoming difficulties on the route. John's task seemed a humbler one, though no less necessary. Bringing up the rear, he insured the safety of the weakest members and thus the integrity of the whole group, whose objective was not to compete but to experience in a literal and immediate way what it means to be all in it together as members of one body. Both the leader and the person at the rear were engaged in pastoral care; their work, though they may not have thought of it in these terms at the time, was to be present in some of the ways Christ is present, before us and behind us.

The Christ who is "behind me" is the Christ who guards my back. In my reading about dreams, and in my experience of them, it has become clear to me how many classic fear dreams feature dangerous pursuers—shadowy figures who are after us, bearing weapons, bearing down upon us until we wake, sweating and relieved. The fear of danger from behind, from stalkers, predators, and spies, fuels the vast industry of thrillers and espionage movies. The hero often discovers danger at the climactic moment, in the rearview mirror.

One of the most dramatic stories in the Old Testament—the flight of the Israelites from Pharaoh's army—comes to its climax when God, who has gone before his wandering people, moves to protect them from behind. In Exodus 14 we read:

Then the angel of God, who had been traveling in front of Israel's army, withdrew and went behind them. The pillar of cloud also moved from in front and stood behind them, coming between the armies of Egypt and Israel. Throughout the night the cloud brought darkness to the one side and light to the other side; so neither went near the other all night long.

vv. 19–20

The God who leads goes before. The God who protects goes behind, to shield, defend, and hide those who are seeking escape from the enemy.

A number of other stories make a similar point about the importance of God's protection of the rear flank— God as rear guard. In the story of Jonathan's military victories in 1 Samuel 14, we read that Jonathan's armor bearer climbed the hills right behind him and backed him up as he attacked the Philistines (v. 13). Similarly, in 2 Samuel, Benjamin's men rally behind Abner to back him up as he goes into battle (2:25). When David leads his six hundred men through the Besor Ravine, some stay behind to guard the way of escape and forfend pursuers—a group as important to victory as those who follow their leader into battle (1 Sam. 30:9). It may seem alien to many of us now to think of God's action in terms of such military metaphors, but still they invite us to reflect on battle as an image of our situation on earth, where spiritual and political warfare continue.

They also remind us how constantly we need to seek and count on God's presence and protection. Like Moses and like Jonathan, we may find ourselves at times in positions of leadership when it seems there is no one to follow, no guide scoping out the uncertain territory ahead, no clear direction. At those times, it is good to remember that sometimes Christ, our brother, our leader, our guide and captain, goes behind us, allowing us to grow in wisdom and trust and confidence by stepping up to the front line. There, if we fall, we fall back into his arms and into his protection. Knowing we have a "backup" gives us confidence to make the leaps of faith that might seem foolish. Though there may be real risk, there is also real protection from ultimate loss.

The fact that we have eyes only in the front of our heads may seem a design flaw, but it also keeps us deeply, physically dependent on one another; others can always see something we can't. To know that Christ stands behind us is to know that, in an ultimate way, we are safe. We are predators, to be sure, but also prey. As prey we know ourselves to be vulnerable to pursuit and attack, and in need at all times of one who can see what we can't. Knowing that, we are free to direct our energies to what is given us to see and attend to. Our rear is guarded. One walks behind us, unhurried, willing to stop with us when we are weary, keeping us from unseen dangers, patient with our slowest pace, ready to lighten our load when it becomes too heavy.

Another way to understand the metaphor of the Lord as the one who goes behind is to consider the agricultural images that occur so frequently in Scripture. In 1 Samuel 11 we read of Saul returning from the fields behind his oxen. Saul is the one who guides the animal in its work, places it under the yoke, and directs its course. There is work for the ox to do, but it is the farmer, the landowner, who designs the work and trains the ox to appropriate labor. The "Lord of the Harvest" guides us in his furrows.

We find another image of the Lord as the one who follows in 2 Kings, when a king sends a messenger ahead of him to the prophet Elisha. Elisha recognizes in the messenger a harbinger of the one who follows: "Is not the sound of his master's footsteps behind him?" he asks (2 Kings 6:32). The master follows the servant, who prepares the way for him. So when we hear, "Prepare ye the way of the Lord," we know that where we go, the Master will follow. This is how God consents to work with us: allowing us to open paths and sites and minds and hearts for his Spirit and Word to enter. Thinking of our work in this way—as preparation for the work of Christ who follows where we take him—assigns a high responsibility to us as messengers and heralds and scouts and explorers, and sometimes as prophets.

Isaiah makes this relationship explicit in his description of the communion between the prophet and the God who guides him: "Whether you turn to the right or to the left, your ears will hear a voice behind you, saying, 'This is the way; walk in it'" (Isa. 30:21). Ezekiel likewise hears the voice of the Spirit coming from behind him: "The Spirit lifted me up, and I heard behind me a loud rumbling sound—May the glory of the LORD be praised in his dwelling place!" (Ezek. 3:12). The voice coming from behind is a prompt, gentle coaching, sometimes still and small, from One who allows us to confront the world unimpeded and view the whole horizon of possibilities, but who helps us find direction among them, if we listen. Or it overtakes us, as it does John when, as he writes in the book of Revelation, "On the Lord's Day I was in the Spirit, and I heard behind me a loud voice like a trumpet" (1:10). The one who comes from behind takes us by surprise—sometimes shocks us into attention.

When Jesus invokes the image of the yoke ("Take my yoke upon you and learn from me" [Matt. 11:29]) it is to make clear that the role of the one who imposes the yoke is to train and teach. He will guide us in the right paths, walking behind, steadying the yoke that burdens us just enough to discipline us to our calling. "For my yoke is easy," he promises, "and my burden is light" (Matt. 11:30). Paul takes up this image of the yoke in various places, addressing a member of the church at Philippi as a loyal "yokefellow" in recognition of their shared relationship to the master who holds the reins and guides the plow. Walking behind us, he trains us to a task larger than we can or need to comprehend. Our part is faithfully to walk the path he sets and to walk in step with our "yokefellows," conspiring (a word that literally means "breathing together") joyfully as we go.

Agricultural life offers another image of the one who walks behind in the story of Ruth, who walks behind the harvesters to gather the wheat left for the poor. The gleaner, gathering what is left over after the harvest, situates herself humbly with those who depend on others' bounty. Farmers in the Israelite community were obliged to leave a portion of their grain for just this purpose. Ruth, walking behind them, accepts the benefit of their bounty. When he identifies with "the least of these," Christ aligns himself with the poor. He reminds us that those who walk behind us, taking the leftovers we donate to charity, eating the food gleaned from restaurants and grocery stores after the affluent have shopped and eaten, are those we have always with us, whose welfare is always linked inextricably with ours. If we do not make ourselves aware of those who walk behind us, we lose our anchor in the life of the whole community and forfeit opportunities to practice love. If we do not understand the importance of walking behind and receiving, we forfeit a chance to learn humility. Ruth, walking behind Boaz, finds her beloved. Their love story, which has its place in the lineage of Jesus, offers lessons not only in humility but also in boldness, trust, and initiative. Ruth chooses carefully whom she will follow: "Let me go to the fields," she says to Naomi, "and pick up the leftover grain behind anyone in whose eyes I find favor" (Ruth 2:2). So, too, the Christ who follows us awaits our notice and seeks our love.

The Christ who walks behind gathers what we scatter even when it is not ripe grain but the detritus of broken promises and failures and poor choices. The sins of some, Paul writes to Timothy, "trail behind them" (1 Tim. 5:24), becoming consequential and evident only later to those who come after and suffer their effects. Christ walks behind us to pick up the pieces, to suffer with those who suffer from our poor choices, and to transform broken shards into blessing, bringing good out of evil as only he can.

Walking behind, Christ assumes, in the person of the least of these, the role of the woman who approaches Jesus to be healed by touching the hem of his garment. She comes up behind him, surreptitiously reaches out, and, touching the edge of his cloak, is healed (Luke 8). The woman knows how to access the power available in Jesus. We need not assume he was wholly unaware of her, and yet when he asks "Who touched me?" we know that he has allowed himself to be vulnerable to even this kind of demand. When someone approaches us from behind in this way—the child or student or client who seems almost manipulative in their stratagems for getting what they want—we may do well to recall this story and remember that this, too, may be one of those who come as angels or instruments of Christ, to stretch and try our charity and our willingness to stop and turn and attend to need.

In the story of Simon of Cyrene, we find one of the most moving images of one who walks behind. As the Roman soldiers lead Jesus to his execution, they seize Simon, apparently at random, and make him carry the cross behind Jesus (Luke 23:26). He is recruited to help bear one of the heaviest burdens in history. In consenting to that hard task, Simon becomes another figure of Christ, who, when he asks us to take up our crosses and follow him, promises, even in the asking, to walk behind us as Simon did, and lighten the weight, following us on whatever journey and end await us.

The Christ who walks behind us is also the one who walks before, and who upholds us from beneath and shelters us from above. Perhaps the loveliest reminder of the God "whose center is everywhere and whose periphery is nowhere" comes in the radical reassurances of Psalm 139 where the psalmist sings—in gratitude and relief, and with deepening confidence—"You hem me in—behind and before; you have laid your hand upon me." Behind us, he follows and gathers, he watches and protects, he waits for us to find our way, he guides without controlling, he prompts and directs, and he carries the heaviest part of the crosses we may think we carry alone. Like the person climbing the mountain with the slowest on the trail, he leaves no one behind but waits in divine patience—who has all the time in the world—for the strength that will come as we grow in the Spirit to the point when we can run and not be weary. And when we mount up with wings like eagles, on his strength and in his good time, he will be there, moving the currents that bear us heavenward.

4

Christ Before Me

Wherever you go, God got there first and is waiting for you. This assurance, beautifully developed in Psalm 139, opens the widest possible space for adventure. There is nowhere I can go where I am unobserved, unprotected, unanticipated. In the psalm, this includes descending into the pit of hell. I am never out of God's reach and never in a situation God doesn't know intimately, personally, because he's "been there" before me—an assurance that echoes Moses's promise to the anxious Israelites: "The LORD himself goes before you and will be with you; he will never leave you nor forsake you. Do not be afraid; do not be discouraged" (Deut. 31:8).

As a child I loved the story of the Israelites in the desert, led by a pillar of cloud by day and a pillar of fire by night. Aided by a flannel board and two large "pillars" of sticky paper, I came to understand that God could appear in any fashion and lead by any means. I also loved stories about angels appearing along dark paths, and lights of unknown source that guided the lost through the forest—and more than those rather sentimental nineteenth-century images, the Exodus angel story where God promises Moses, "Now go, lead the people to the place I spoke of, and my angel will go before you" (Exod. 32:34). The God who guides and goes before seemed to me both reassuring and unpredictable. This God could appear as a friend, a stranger, or a phenomenon of nature. The core truth, in all such stories, is that we are led.

As I got older and "put away childish things" (1 Cor. 13:11) (well . . . some of them), I acquired my own skepticism about people's claims to have been "led" to do what, coincidentally, was also to their obvious benefit. It is easy to be deceived about what we feel "led" to do. Whether it is, in fact, God who is leading is always a matter to be carefully discerned. Not to mistake my own superficial desires for the leadings of Christ requires that I remain humbly aware of what tends to lead me astray and, like an airline pilot, constantly correct my course by reattuning my heart to the guidance available in Scripture and the promptings of the Spirit.

I am often struck in rereading the Gospels by what appears to have been Jesus' habitual attunement to the voice of the Father. He seems always to have been "listening in" for God's voice. I know people who do this. They are deeply countercultural in that they seem more interested in being good followers than in being leaders. Especially among those who seek to inspire the young, "leadership" has become something of a buzzword—an objective held out to all on the dubious premise that we can all be leaders. While every one of us may develop certain leadership skills, being a good follower, especially understanding what it means to follow Christ, requires a different idea of excellence and a different kind of hope.

One pastor I know describes himself routinely not with the adjective "Christian" but with the full phrase "a follower of Jesus." Following Jesus has led him into some dangerous and life-changing places. Though he is a known leader, it is as a follower that he most deeply understands his calling. The follower doesn't focus primarily on taking initiative, staying "proactive," or staying "ahead of the curve" or "at the cutting edge," much as we applaud those virtues in this competitive culture. The follower stays in relationship with a leader he trusts, watching, listening, loving, taking the next step as the path unfolds, saying yes. The life of the follower, provided it is Christ who leads, is likely to be every bit as adventurous and empowering as that of a self-styled leader. In the same spirit in which Paul asked, "If God is for us, who can be against us?" (Rom. 8:31) we might ask, "If Christ go before us, who can lead us astray?"

Behind that rhetorical question lies a whole history of learning. It was not always self-evident to the Israelites milling about under the burning desert sun, unemployed, uncertain of their future, and unconvinced that Moses wasn't a madman, that their journey through the wilderness was a divine mission. Such doubts are familiar to most of us in those times when it is not altogether clear that our fidelities are "paying off" in security, satisfaction, or advancement in holiness—quite the contrary. In those periods it is good both to review the long history of God's work and to take the larger view: that God acts in history, that Christ leads us straight to the cross, that at the end of that sorrowful road and at the other side of the Valley of the Shadow lies good news, that in life and death, we are the Lord's.

This is the great paradox of Christian faith: Christ's death is our way to life. The bad news is the good news. "I go to prepare a place for you" (John 14:2 ESV), Jesus told the disciples, and we, after them, cling to that promise as we walk toward the cross along our own winding paths. God has gone before us from the very beginning of the story, subduing the land "before the people of Israel" (Num. 32:4), preparing the hearts of those to whom the prophets delivered their unpopular messages, making a path through the waters and escape routes in battle, and putting threatening enemies to sleep.

The God of space who leads us through this "vale" is also the God of time, who has gone before us in history and inhabits the future—the One "who was and is and is to come" (Rev. 4:8). "I tell you the truth," Jesus says, "before Abraham was born, I am!" (John 8:58). Those who "search for the historical Jesus" may be baffled by claims that locate him, and us, in the paradox of coexistence in timelessness and time. He is the God for whom, as T. S. Eliot put it, "All is always now."[1] He "prevents us everywhere," meaning he precedes and anticipates us. "Before they call I will answer," the Lord tells Isaiah (Isa. 65:24), and the psalmist, who knows this, writes a hymn of reassurance in recognition of how fully God, who himself is timeless, knows us in our mortal state, bound by time: "Before a word is on my tongue, you know it completely, O Lord" (Ps. 139:4). And Jesus echoes them: "Your Father knows what you need before you ask him" (Matt. 6:8).

All these testimonies to God's foreknowledge invite us to a larger understanding of the God who dwells outside time and history. Mystics and poets as well as prophets have tried for centuries to find a language to express the "eternal nowness" of the life of the Trinity. But our language is as time-bound as we are, and so we resort to temporal terms that stretch to the limits of our imagination to open up the mystery of the One who is, and who was, and who is to come. He gave us his own name in the eternal present: I AM. Throughout the Gospel of John we hear Jesus reiterate that mysterious self-identification: I AM. And so it is as one who is present to us in every moment that Christ goes before us, leading, guiding, preparing a way.

But *before* itself is a curious term. Christ not only "goes" before me but also simply "stands" before me—self-revealing, summoning me, stopping me in my tracks, holding me in his burning, loving gaze. David lived in this awareness, and it guided him through battle and into song: "I have set the Lord always before me. Because he is at my right hand, I will not be shaken" (Ps.

16:8). From the burning bush to the transfiguration to Jesus' appearance in the upper room to the ambush on the road to Damascus, Scripture invites us to recognize epiphany as a divine teaching strategy. God stops us in our tracks from time to time and stands before us, making himself manifest in any number of ways. When God threatened punishment for Sodom, Abraham "remained standing before the Lord" (Gen. 18:22) and pled for the city, bargaining for its survival with a God who listened and allowed his servant his say—and who did not destroy the city, because his mercy was greater than his will for vengeance.

The same God appears before Moses, speaking from the burning bush. "Take off your sandals," God tells him, "for the place where you are standing is holy ground" (Exod. 3:5). In that simple act of removing his sandals, Moses acquiesces not only to a gesture of appropriate humility but also to the clear message that he wasn't going anywhere until the God who blazed before him released him.

In a similar way, Jesus stands before Peter, James, and John, transfigured. "His face shone like the sun, and his clothes became as white as the light." And a voice from heaven speaks to the bewildered witnesses: "This is my Son, whom I love; with him I am well pleased. Listen to him!" (Matt. 17:2, 5). These revelations happen at still points in the journey. The Christ who has traveled dusty roads side by side with his followers occasionally steps into the path, unveiled, and draws them suddenly and shockingly into a new level of awareness and relationship.

He does not always come transfigured by fire or light, or on a mountaintop. Sometimes he appears before us as unexceptionally as a street person or student or neighbor. (I think particularly of some of the homeless on our streets who so often say "God bless you" even to those who pass without offering help.) Sometimes he comes as a numinous presence in the midst of prayer. Sometimes he awakens us by means of a phrase of music, a line of poetry, or an image.

I remember standing before a Russian icon in the Metropolitan Museum of Art some time ago. I had been touring the room, as one does in museums, letting my eye alight on one image after another, lingering here and there to gaze a little longer. Then my eye was caught—forcibly, as I recall—by a portrait of Christ, whose piercing gaze summoned me from the other side of the large room. I crossed to stand in front of it, moved, mystified, a little unsettled by the powerful sense of being addressed, confronted, called into the presence of a God who calls us personally to account.

Having been raised with a certain theological prejudice against the use of images in worship, I was not sure at the time what to make of an experience that felt like a real encounter with a Christ really present, there in the museum. I was facing an icon displayed, after all, not as an object of veneration but as a part of an art exhibition. Since then, I have learned a little more about the role of icons in Orthodox worship, and have come to respect the ways they serve, as do other arts, to give us access to the God who awaits us everywhere, just behind the veil.

"Before our eyes the Lord sent miraculous signs and wonders," the writer of Deuteronomy records (6:22). And he still does, though we do not always read the signs or wonder enough. In nature as well as art, we are addressed, tenderly, faithfully, subtly.

"Subtle is the Lord," said Einstein, who bore more witness than most to the Lord's subtleties. What lies before us in all the objects and movements in our visual field is fraught with mystery enough for a lifetime of reflection. Remembering that, we can look around and say with the psalmist, "Your love is ever before me, and I walk continually in your truth" (Ps. 26:3). All our walking takes us in the direction of a Love that waits for us. Wherever we seek him, we will find ourselves face-to-face with One who went before us to prepare a place, who stands before us to summon us into communion, and who walks before us to lead us home.

5

CHRIST BESIDE ME

T he original text of St. Patrick's prayer, in place of "Christ beside me," reads "Christ on my right, Christ on my left." Cecil Alexander in 1889 compressed the two lines in the hymn version, sacrificing the explicit reminder that Christ flanks us on both sides. He who "sitteth on the right hand of God the Father," as the creed tells us, stands ready at our "right hand" as well. The symbolism of the right hand (with due apologies to lefties) has traditionally suggested priority. The loyalty, competency, and indispensability of the "right-hand man" (even if she's a woman) is unquestioned.

Christ on my left invokes the archetype of the "left hand" of darkness, the shadow side, the unconscious, the instinctual, the intuitive. The image of Christ on my left carries a symbolic suggestion of a helper who works in and with and through us in ways that may not even reach our full awareness. He speaks to us in our dreams and in our wandering thoughts, in sudden noticings and in the unbidden "Aha!" moments that lift us to a new level of understanding. He is a partner more intimate with our hidden selves than a spouse or a brother.

The idea of our being empowered to collaborate with Christ accents God's condescension in the best sense: God descends in order to be with us and to work with us, making us co-workers in bringing the divine plan into being. Such a partnership reminds me of what it means to ask one of the four-year-olds I love for their help. I ask them for two reasons; needing their actual help is generally not one of them. I ask them because I want and value their companionship, and I am aware that in asking them I am offering them a chance to learn. Sitting at their sides, working with them at their pace, I am slowed into love that has no agenda but delight.

A pastor friend of mine who spends much of his time working with people emerging from trauma frequently describes his work as "coming alongside." He doesn't impose an agenda, enter into lives uninvited, or give unsolicited advice, but he shows up, sits with, walks with, prays with, and stands in solidarity with them in their trouble and sorrow. This is the work of the Christ who walked with disciples and among the crowds, sat with them around campfires, and appeared as a companion on the road to Emmaus. He is the one who makes every step of the journey at our sides, known or unrecognized. The Christ who walks beside me sees, adopts, and knows my perspective. The point of the incarnation is this: that God can and does enter into our point of view and translates the ineffable glory and magnitude of divinity into terms we can grasp.

That grasp depends upon One who understands far more than we do, and who bridges the gap between his perspective and ours. Much recent educational research has focused on "learning styles." Teachers are encouraged to recognize and adapt to different students' needs for different kinds of instruction, roughly categorized as visual, auditory, or tactile. Various "type indicators" like the Myers-Briggs Type Indicator or Multiple Intelligence Models have been developed to identify variations in the ways people process new information. The point of such instruments and the studies they have enabled is to allow us to "come alongside" each other more effectively as we participate in teaching and learning. But their effectiveness depends on the deeper intention, not just to catalogue and identify, but to draw near and enter into the intimate process of another person's life and growth, asking, "Who are you? What is it like to be you? What kind of loving care do you need? What kind of healing? What fears need to be dispelled before you can open your heart and mind?" Coming alongside in this way involves just the kind of reassurance we see in so many biblical stories of encounters with divine messengers: "Be not afraid."

For small children, the surest comfort and antidote to nighttime fears is the parent who stays beside them as they let sleep come. After all the bedtime rituals, the stories, the prayers, the lullabies, what remains is simply presence. And as children grow older, no longer needing the explicit comforts of infancy, too big to be carried, still the parent who walks beside them into their first classroom, who walks beside the wobbling bike, who sits beside them as they puzzle over math problems or stands at the counter as they crack their first eggs and beat them offers something no amount of verbal instruction could achieve. It is a ministry of presence. It is the best we can offer children, and also the best we can offer those who mourn, those who are sick or dying, those who are mired in confusion. It is the heart of pastoral care. It is a humble, human-sized imitation of Christ, who walks beside us, empowering us with unutterable love.

In the ritual and iconography of the Old Testament world, standing beside betokened a very particular relationship and set of responsibilities. Officers and trumpeters stood beside the king to reinforce, celebrate, and proclaim his authority (see 2 Kings 11:14). His queen sat at his side to share and consolidate his power. Elders surrounded King David in his grief when he lost a child, and soldiers went beside him in battle. A heavenly being stood beside Shadrach, Meshach, and Abednego in the fiery furnace to accompany and protect them, and a "man" stood beside Ezekiel as he listened to a voice from heaven. The throne of King Solomon was flanked by lions on each side, signs of power and protection. In both Old and New Testaments, angels come to stand beside God's chosen at crucial moments—when Christ ascends to heaven, when sight is restored to the stricken Saul, when Paul faced trial before Caesar. And always, in biblical literature and in stories of every culture, the position of the special friend and companion, the "sidekick" who offers comfort, counsel, amusement, and insight is lifted up in recognition of the fact that, in friendship as well as in marriage, "it is not good that the man should be alone" (Gen. 2:18 ESV). Moses and Aaron, David and Jonathan, Ruth and Naomi, Paul and Barnabas offer us ways of understanding the rich complexity of what we call friendship, and of what spiritual companionship may require: compensations for the other's weakness; shared secrets and shared risk; leaving home for another's sake; sharing perils and persecutions for the sake of a shared faith and mutual trust.

Centuries of story have continued to explore and expand this theme of walking beside. Don Quixote has Sancho Panza to keep him grounded in practical common sense as he pursues a great dream. King Lear has his faithful servant, Kent. Melville's Ishmael has Queequeg, a vivid reminder that "civilized" white culture has no monopoly on kindness and courage. Huck Finn has Jim, the runaway slave who shares his raft and who, risking far more than the white boy, loves and teaches him from a point of view no other adult could give him. Frodo has Sam, a hero in his own right, whose service on a perilous journey is indispensable to its completion. And, in another vein, Hester Prynne has Pearl, the child always at her side, who both manifests her sin and mitigates readers' judgments of it. The one who walks beside may serve many roles: shadow, conscience, counterpart, teacher, trickster, comforter. The Christ who walks beside may take on these roles and others: empowering, restraining, revealing, directing, or simply waiting for us to find our way.

It is one thing to wait while someone goes off and returns. It is another to enter into the journey as a companion, consenting to go along even on perilous and foolhardy excursions. "If I make my bed in the depths, you are there," the psalmist marvels. "If I rise on the wings of the dawn, if I settle on the far side of the sea, even there your hand will guide me, your right hand will hold me fast" (Ps. 139:8–10). This is not the top-down guidance of an authoritarian or agenda-driven manager, but rather the patient, watchful oversight of a loving companion who will walk through anything we need to do in the course of learning to be God-awakened, God-centered, fully human beings.

Francis Thompson's stirring poem "The Hound of Heaven" imagines God's pursuit of us as that of an experienced hunter who follows the wayward soul "down the nights and down the days," "down the arches of the years," and "down the labyrinthine ways / Of [his] own mind." It chronicles the long flight and the many attempts to evade "this tremendous Lover" until, in the end, the speaker turns and hears and heeds the invitation, so full of amazing grace, "Rise, clasp My hand, and come."[1] The welcome extended is that of one who offers and emphasizes companionship rather than punishment, recrimination, or even the propriety of penance. It is an invitation very like the one another poet, George Herbert, imagines in a similar poem about spiritual resistance where, after much hesitation to accept the gracious hospitality of a Love who chooses to invite the most unworthy, the two final lines give a simple and moving account of the kind of obedience that brings us into fellowship with Christ: "'You must sit down,' says Love, 'and taste my meat.' So I did sit and eat."[2]

The image of Christ as one who sits beside us at table recalls, of course, the many shared meals in the Gospels when he "did sit and eat" with his followers. On the hillside, sharing the miraculous loaves and fish; in the homes of the wealthy, where he reclined and told pointed stories; at Cana, where he shared a wedding feast; at the Last Supper, where the disciples gathered for a shared meal of whose ultimate significance they were still unaware; at Emmaus, where, seated at a common table, he rocked the very foundations of their understanding. All these moments of divine revelation come not as lightning flashes from a mountaintop but as intimate moments of participation in the most ordinary ritual of human fellowship—eating together. God has many avenues of approach, but it seems the one most preferred is the intimate encounter that takes place as he comes "alongside" us in the midst of what we so blindly call our "ordinary" moments. He comes as the "least of these." "Often and often and often," reads the final line of the ancient Celtic "Rune of Hospitality," "comes the Christ in the guise of a stranger."

Often, and often, as well, Christ communicates with us in other life forms—in the "still waters" beside which we are led, in the "green pastures" in which we lie down, in the "river" beside which Israel's tents spread out like a garden. The very first psalm promises that the righteous man shall be "like a tree, planted by streams of water, which yields its fruit in season and whose leaf does not wither. Whatever he does prospers" (Ps. 1:3). And Isaiah promises the people of God, "They will neither hunger nor thirst, nor will the desert heat or the sun beat upon them. He who has compassion on them will guide them and lead them beside springs of water" (Isa. 49:10). In the same way that the one who feeds us also becomes our food, the one who leads us to springs of water, and promises living water, is in fact what we thirst for.

Biologically speaking, proximities matter immensely: plants need water sources; those next to rivers and streams cannot live without them, and even the hardiest cactus depends upon the deep aquifers that satisfy their slow thirst. Gardeners learn which vegetables "like" to be next to others, which tend to shelter their neighbors, which cross-pollinate, which will draw beneficial insects.

Like plants, when we locate ourselves and find our place on earth, one of the most important pieces of information we need is who our neighbors are. These are people among whom we hope to flourish, and our mere proximity puts us in a situation of interdependence. Those who live beside me will have needs that impinge on mine and gifts to exchange with me. They are the ones through whom I will encounter Christ, and who will provide my most immediate answer to the ancient question, "Who is my neighbor?" Though Christian teaching has expanded the concept of "neighbor" to be far more inclusive than the reach of our immediate neighborhoods, "neighborhood" is still a crucial idea. Far-flung as families are in American culture, most of us have learned to live on at least two levels of connection—the ties that bind us to family and friends around the world are deepened and enhanced by all the electronic aids that keep us "in touch." But at another level, we do have to share our streets and tax base and trash service and weather warnings with the people right beside us. In the midst of floods and hurricanes, in the wake of earthquakes and fallen bridges, in drought and threat of spreading wildfires, the one I find myself beside is my neighbor, indeed. Accounts of mutual aid, even to the point of radical self-sacrifice, always emerge from major disasters like the tsunami or Hurricane Katrina. They remind us that the love Christ embodied and taught is real, present, and available in human community wherever ego and appetite haven't drowned out the still, small voice that calls us to be God's agents on earth and, standing beside one another, to remember our common heritage as God's children.

And that is where we stand, as God's children—beside each other, and beside the Christ who has promised to be our companion on the journey. In the midst of an argument about who would be greatest in the kingdom of heaven, Jesus "took a little child and had him stand beside him," and said to the disputing disciples, "Whoever welcomes this little child in my name welcomes . . . the one who sent me" (Luke 9:47). Standing at Christ's side like that little child, we find our protection and validation, our true identity, and welcome, indeed.

6

CHRIST TO WIN ME

For I, unless thou enthrall me, never shall be free, /
nor ever chaste, except thou ravish me."[1] So ends
John Donne's "Holy Sonnet XIV," an extraordinary
prayer in which the speaker urges God to wrest him from
the enemy who has captured him in battle and holds him
with a grip that only the Almighty is able to break. The
imagery in the poem is extreme; it is up to God to do
battle and win us over, and to "enthrall" or enslave us
to keep us from our wicked and addictive ways. Donne

was a Reformation poet and preacher. His own notorious temptations of the flesh, whose urgencies he recorded in remarkable poems, competed with a desire for God that was just as great—ultimately greater. And he knew the battle with sin would have to be won by a force more powerful than his own will.

In English the word *win* is used most commonly in two contexts: battle or contest, and courtship. A third meaning, ancient but applicable, is to till the ground, or more broadly, to bring about gain by labor. All these uses of the word converge on the idea of gaining something worth great effort. For centuries Christian theologians have argued about the question of what one must do to be saved. At one extreme are those with long check-lists of particulars, beginning with baptism, words of confession and repentance, various forms of penance, attendance at services, and receiving the sacraments at the appointed times. At the other extreme are those who put their whole trust in the mercy of God and who believe (as Martin Luther also did) that, since we very likely break every one of the commandments every day, it is impossible for us to win the battle against evil, and Christ must do it for us. This, they believe, is the whole message of atonement: he has accomplished all that is needful for our salvation and reconciled us to God. Our appropriate response is gratitude and consent—and obedience, as a consequence of that gratitude, but without legalistic anxiety.

In my formative years I was quite confused on the matter of effort as a dimension of spiritual life. Despite the generous efforts of Sunday school teachers, parents, pastors, and youth leaders, I remained, until well into adulthood, uncertain about my assignment: how much "work" was required of me, and what if I didn't do it? The basic theological truth that Jesus had already accomplished my justification and "won" my salvation didn't quite clarify what my job was. I had my own demons, and wrestled with them, sometimes in prayer, sometimes in late-night bouts of anxiety. But Scripture and hymns brought me back to this point: "The strife is o'er, the battle done, / The victory of life is won; / The song of triumph has begun. Alleluia!"[2] The problem, it seemed, was the verb tenses. St. Patrick elides the issue with infinitives (appropriately enough)—"Christ to win me" leaves room for some speculation about when and how the winning takes place (or took place or will take place). The one way out of the struggle is to broach the mystery of timelessness implied in God's very name: I AM. Christ has won me, continues to win me, does battle for me daily.

And that's very good news. But the battle imagery takes me only so far. If not an absolute pacifist, I nevertheless find it very hard to believe that any war solves anything for long, that war should ever be anything but a last resort, or that the "holy war" language we have used for so long to justify greed and slaughter is more than a thin mask. So the metaphor has its limitations, at least for my twenty-first-century imagination, darkened by the wars my generation has witnessed. Even the scriptural idea of "spiritual warfare," important as it is, may be a metaphor for a process of transformation beyond the capacity of human categories to describe. We resort to images of war because they are available to describe the work of a heavenly plan and the exercise of divine power that lie beyond history but unfold in human history in ways that are riddled with ambiguity.

So I reach back to the more ancient idea embedded in the word *winning*—plowing the ground, laboring for a harvest. Here, too, the old hymns led me into some confusion. One of the faithful at Wednesday night prayer meetings persisted in choosing the stolid nineteenth-century hymn, full of determination and admonishment, "Work, for the night is coming, / work through the morning hours, / work while the dew is sparkling, / work 'mid springing flowers, / work when the day grows brighter, / work in the glowing sun; / work, for the night is coming,

/ when man's work is done."[3] The text is based on John 9:4–5, where Jesus, in the midst of healing a blind man, says to the disciples, "As long as it is day, we must do the work of him who sent me. Night is coming, when no one can work. While I am in the world, I am the light of the world." But the hymn's emphatic and rather relentless repetition of the imperative to work would leave me, many a Wednesday night, feeling a kind of spiritual exhaustion. My mother, an energetic, lively, loving missionary and later deacon in our church, had no problem with work. She had worked all her life, understood the call to a life of service, and found her deepest satisfactions in the classic works of mercy: teaching, visiting the sick, feeding the hungry, caring for the poor and the downcast—and also preparing food for countless potluck suppers, baking communion bread, housing visiting speakers, and sharing her home with foster children. The examples she set leave me much to be grateful for and to try to live up to. Nevertheless, there is a point all believers must come to when we become aware that Christ has already completed our incomplete work. Then we are freed to take our rest in him, confident that salvation is not all up to us.

Every farmer knows this: there is the time of waiting after planting that provides a long reminder that human work is absolutely contingent on forces we cannot control, try as we might—on what Dylan Thomas beautifully called "the force that through the green fuse drives the flower."[4] The parable of the kingdom of heaven in Mark 4 is perfectly explicit on this point:

> This is what the kingdom of God is like. A man scatters seed on the ground. Night and day, whether he sleeps or gets up, the seed sprouts and grows, though he does not know how. All by itself the soil produces grain— first the stalk, then the head, then the full kernel in the head. As soon as the grain is ripe, he puts the sickle to it, because the harvest has come.
>
> vv. 26–29

Christ, Lord of the harvests, does that work of germination, in the soil and in our souls, in ways of which we cannot, and need not, be fully aware. Sometimes we are confronted and summoned. Sometimes we are simply allowed to live in this world, moving among its many currents, and to learn.

And here is what the Scriptures and the world teach us all in time: that we live among both wheat and tares, and for the time being, both flourish. That we dwell in paradoxes that will not be resolved in this life. That there are more things in heaven and earth than we have dreamt of, that learning takes courage, and that the best of us venture out to the learning edge, willing to leave the comfort zone for the sake of truth. And that our search for truth, if we are faithful to it, will lead us to the threshold of mystery where the appetite for certainty gives way to humility and awe.

My part, then, is to consent to the terms of that search, and to stay in relationship with the one who is the Truth (and the Way, and the Life), and to say yes to his invitations as well as his challenges. He wins the battle with the powers of darkness; he also wins my heart like the "tremendous Lover" in Francis Thompson's poem where Christ woos and pursues with almost frightening persistence. The image of courtship has equal roots in Scripture with that of battle: Christ is the Bridegroom who came to seek us and win our hearts. "From Heaven he came and sought us, to be his holy bride," the hymn reminds us, with the kind of self-sacrificial love Paul holds up as a model for husbands who should "love your wives, just as Christ loved the church" (Eph. 5:25).[5]

The Bridegroom, to woo and win, watches and follows and argues and entices. Christ, the Bridegroom in Thompson's poem, is not the abject, rejected lover of so much Renaissance verse, but one who is as confident as he is eager to win the faint-hearted, fleeing beloved. "I fled him," the poem begins.[6] The speaker not only flees, but hides, seeks asylum at "the margent of the world" and in the recesses of nature where he begs evening to come soon and "with thy young skyey blossoms heap me over / from this tremendous Lover." But he finds that nature "cannot slake my drouth." He tempts the faithful to take sides with him, and looks for allies even among children, but they evade him. The poem keeps up a breathless account of flight and pursuit, lovely but disturbing in its elaboration of the fear that drives one from Christ. Still, at intervals it comes to rest on the reassurance that "fear wist not to evade as love wist to pursue" (which is to say, love is better at pursuing than fear is at evading); Christ's love is stronger and more persistent than our fears. This, too, is very good news.

The last section of the poem begins with a vivid surrender: "Naked I wait thy Love's uplifted stroke!"—a line that expresses the radical and certain character of Christ's love by borrowing, like Donne, an image of violence. Indeed, when the "tremendous Lover" speaks again, it is not sweetly but with a voice not unlike the God who thundered in response to Job's complaint. "Strange, piteous, futile thing!" he says, "Wherefore should any set thee love apart? . . . How hast thou merited— / Of all man's clotted clay the dingiest clot? / Alack, thou knowest not / How little worthy of love thou art!"[7] Hard as it may be to imagine such a comeuppance as a winning strategy, it is exactly that, because it rings so soundly of a core truth about who the Lover is in relation to the beloved, what he offers, and what it is worth. Moreover, it is followed by what in context might seem the unlikeliest kind of invitation: "Rise, clasp My hand, and come!"

Despite the antiquity of its language and a number of arcane symbols, the poem has appealed widely to readers over the past century because there is comfort value in recognizing the biblical truth that often gets lost in religious rhetoric about how "I" found God or came to Christ. *He* is the one who finds *us*, woos us, wins us, prepares a home for us, gathers us into his care. And, oddly, in a sense, we are the prize. That we are so loved is amazing, indeed. That the Creator delights in his creatures, that Christ desires our company and calls us friends, seems at times one of the most counterintuitive tenets of Christian teaching.

The English poet U. A. Fanthorpe attests wittily to the remarkable character of Christ's unlikely love in her poem "Getting It Across," where Jesus, the speaker, ruefully takes stock of the rabble he's chosen for disciples. "These numskulls are my medium," he muses. "I called them."[8] Even in their density, their competitiveness, their moments of greed, their doubt, he loves them. In Acts and the subsequent history of the early church, we see the flowering of that love in them.

We, too, have been chosen, fought for, worked for, wooed, and won. In her delightful account of working with small children in Sunday school, Anne Lamott describes an exercise with which her classes begin. One by one the children are surprised by a very particular summons: "Is anyone wearing a blue sweatshirt with a Pokémon on it?" Those who, to their surprise, meet the criteria come forward and are greeted with "You are so loved and so chosen." One child, having found himself among this privileged, swelling crowd, "clutched at himself like a beauty pageant finalist."[9] The message, no matter how often it is repeated, retains its amazing quality: you are so loved, and so chosen. And we are. Anyone wearing a Pokémon sweatshirt. Or bare feet. Or jeans. Or pinstripes. Or saris or hijabs. Anyone fleeing or fighting or fearful. We are so chosen. We have been called by name, and we are his.

CHRIST TO COMFORT
AND RESTORE ME

The very first question in the Heidelberg Catechism, pulling no punches, shocks us into fully reckoning with our human condition before God: "What is thy only comfort in life and death?" The answer offers the deepest reassurance available to Christians in this precarious world:

79

That I with body and soul, both in life and death, am not my own, but belong unto my faithful Saviour Jesus Christ; who, with his precious blood, has fully satisfied for all my sins, and delivered me from all the power of the devil; and so preserves me that without the will of my heavenly Father, not a hair can fall from my head; yea, that all things must be subservient to my salvation, and therefore, by his Holy Spirit, he also assures me of eternal life, and makes me sincerely willing and ready, henceforth, to live unto him.

The comfort Christ offers begins by calling us to look death in the face and take the measure of our own sins and of what they have cost. As Thomas Hardy put it, "If way to the better there be, it exacts a full look at the worst."[1] Having taken that full look, the promise of comfort and restoration is very good news; we are held in the will of a completely attentive God who cares more than we can imagine, and calls us to life, not by avoiding death but by preparing us to walk through it, and through the sufferings that precede it, with full confidence.

"Comfort" and "restore" are not entirely separable ideas. The original meaning of "comfort" was to strengthen. An early rule of religious life enumerates nine "comforts" against temptation; to be comforted was not simply to be made to feel better, or even to be healed from pain or sorrow, but to be equipped to face the next struggle. The word stretched to include encouragement (to be given courage), incitement (to be given motive), aid (to be given help), succor (to be given respite and refreshment), and support (to be accompanied or backed up).

The object of comfort is full restoration; we are brought back wounded and discouraged from our battles to a loving God, brushed off, nourished, and equipped to go forth again, restored to a state of grace and readiness, and given new hope. Sometimes (ancient usage implies) we are even "improved." The Comforter is also the Teacher who can turn our most shameful defeats to good purpose and make them instruments of wisdom.

It has often occurred to me to wonder what kind of life the prodigal son came home to: what lay in store for him after his father's extravagant and merciful welcome? The moment of comfort recorded in Luke's spare story is a sweet one: "But while he was still a long way off, his father saw him and was filled with compassion for him; he ran to his son, threw his arms around him and kissed him" (15:20). Then come the robe, the sandals, the fatted calf, the celebration. Then the envy of the elder brother, who enters the story not only to remind us of the different ways God deals with his children but also to make us aware of the lingering consequences of bad choices—the cleanup work, the task of restoring broken relationships, the guilt, the lost credibility. The work of restoration will take time. Like us, when we fall away, fail, or act foolishly and find ourselves once again repenting, the returned son dwells in the paradox of salvation: it is fully accomplished, as Jesus said on the cross, and yet we remain on a journey and in a historical unfolding that is yet to be completed. The compassionate father (and let us not forget the "motherly" comfort of God implied throughout Scripture) comforts his son and restores him to his place in the family; he equips him to assume that place and to start again. He even, it seems, against all common sense, rewards him. But all this may be necessary strengthening for what is to come—the long work of coming home that only begins when the door, and the father's arms, are flung open.

Restoration is never exactly a return to things as they were. Jesus' promise of comfort to those who mourn has only on a few recorded occasions involved bringing the dead back to this life. That we will meet them again in the next life can seem very cold comfort indeed, when the ache of their departure is fresh, and the outrage that often comes with it. Those very human emotions deserve to be acknowledged and addressed. I learned something valuable about the importance of making room for full expression of pain, loss, grief, and anger from a friend who worked in a battered women's shelter. It is important, she told me, not to urge the women to forgiveness too quickly, or to be too hasty with efforts to bring injured women back to someplace we might recognize as emotional equanimity. The careful, caring work of comforting abused women involved volunteers in listening to their fury, their sobs, their fears, their despair. The first stage of comfort, they learned, was to allow the pain to be fully spoken. Only then, and gradually, could most of the injured begin to imagine a return to lives that felt worthwhile, safe to live, capable of confidence and even joy. Then the work of practical restoration could begin—new jobs, new legal arrangements for children, new circles of trust and support, new ways of claiming faith when old ways proved inadequate to what they had suffered.

From the darkness of the Valley of the Shadow—the injury of abuse, the lingering illness and death, the clinical depression, economic hopelessness, broken relationships—the journey can look bleak, and the terms on which we retain the gift of life, hard indeed. And even comfort exacts a cost. It will not be the comfort we most long for in the moment of loss—the touch of the departed beloved, the sound of a voice or the flash of a smile, or even the ordinary irritations that come in the dailiness of life with the one we have loved, warts and all. It will be something else, more complex and more adequate for this stage of our journey, and more surprising. It may be simply that we feel for the first time the vigor and practical truth of pieties we never had to claim—that even in the pit, in the "uttermost parts of the sea," in the depths of spiritual darkness, we are held by the strong right hand of God. In a poem he wrote to claim, by paraphrase, the reassurances of Psalm 130, Sir Thomas Wyatt records his own encounter with the God of comfort:

> From depth of sin and from a deep despair,
>   From depth of death, from depth of heartes
>   sorrow,
>   From this deep cave of darkness' deep repair,
> Thee have I call'd, O Lord, to be my borow. . . .[2]

The image of God as "my burrow," the place in which I bury my head in shame, the lap into which I nestle like a spent child, the cave in which I hide to lick my wounds and rest, humanly and poignantly indicates what sort of comfort we are inclined to imagine from the grip of exhaustion and despair. I think of the things I want to "burrow" into when I need comfort and restoration. I want to curl up with my husband or, failing that, with a good book. I want to eat a good, simple meal with someone I love, slowly. I want to play, or hear, a few measures of Bach or Schumann. I want to walk in the evening sun.

This line of Wyatt's prayer encourages me to recognize in all those comforts the hand of a gracious and compassionate God who meets me in my daily needs and who not only provides music, food, company, and sunlight but, in a sense, takes on those forms of beauty to be present to me. A lovely line from Nikos Kazanzakis has helped me recognize divine utterance in many small things and made them sources of comfort and restoration: "I said to the almond tree, 'Friend, speak to me of God,' and the almond tree blossomed." God speaks—in the blossoming tree, in the cooling breeze, in the chance encounter (in "mouth of friend and stranger"), in the words and images that arise when we are at prayer. To listen for that speech is not always to cease from ordinary activity, but sometimes to reenter and reframe that activity, and to see in it a new invitation to trust.

Poet and farmer Wendell Berry offers abundant wise counsel and comfort to the many who, like him, mourn the destruction of natural ecosystems and abuse of resources that have resulted from North American habits of overconsumption. He reminds us that we live together in a condition of sin and sickness, chronically in need of repentance, forgiveness, a wider vision of hope, and a deeper understanding of what our spiritual and physical health entails if we are to be restored. His little poem "The Slip," written after he saw a whole acre of valuable, arable land give way and sink into the river, reflects helpfully on how comfort and restoration come in taking a long view of human and divine process:

> The maker moves
> in the unmade, stirring the water until
> it clouds, dark beneath the surface,
> stirring and darkening the soul until pain
> perceives new possibility. There is nothing
> to do but learn and wait, return to work
> on what remains. Seed will sprout in the scar.
> Though death is in the healing, it will heal.[3]

Three truths emerge conspicuously from this little passage that offer a durable way of understanding comfort and restoration: (1) there is nothing to do but learn, wait, and return to work on what remains, (2) seed will sprout in the scar, and (3) healing and death are not always mutually exclusive. The urgency with which we often rush to "do something" in situations of disaster or anguish may need to be tempered by a willingness to wait—for natural processes to take their course, for God to reveal the next step, for the "cooling down" that prudence and wisdom demand. It may strain our patience to accept the doing nothing that is called for; we're conditioned, most of us, to believe that something is better than nothing. But the aftermath of a disaster or loss or failure is precisely the time to "wait on the Lord." And in that waiting, curious forms of comfort and restoration may come: a deepened awareness of the contingency of our lives and fortunes, a new level of trust.

The image of seed sprouting in the scar offers a realistic, practical image of hope that defies false comforts. There will be scarring. The landscape, the body, the psyche, may be permanently changed. There may be a visible mark that lasts for a lifetime. And the new life that comes will not obliterate, but remind us continually of the death that occasioned its coming. Comfort is costly. Sometimes, as we are reminded in the third point made in this little stanza—"death is in the healing." It comes at the cost of death, not only the death that brought on the grief, but in what must die in us in order to open our hearts to the growing involved in restoration.

It is easy, any therapist will tell you, for people to get stuck in and even addicted to their grief. Some people organize their lives and identities around a defining loss, finding in it the false comfort that comes in others' pity. The question that preceded several of Jesus' healings— "Do you want to be healed?"—makes clear that the will to be healed often competes with a perverse desire to cling to our disabling losses and sicknesses. In order to accept the real healing in which lie comfort and restoration, one has to give up false comforts and take a risk. (Monty Python encouraged a healthy amusement at that tendency in a comic depiction of the rueful "ex-leper," healed by Jesus and sent on his way, who suddenly realized he could no longer demand alms of passersby. The necessity of finding another livelihood seriously complicated—and compromised—his gratitude.) Christ the Comforter comes with what one poet called "the sickle of [his] mercy" to call us away from false comforts and into a new set of challenging opportunities for growth.[4] His comfort comes with a call to renewal. It invigorates and summons us to joy, as the psalmist reminds us when he prays, "Restore to me the joy of your salvation and grant me a willing spirit, to sustain me" (Ps. 51:12). This is not too much to ask; it is exactly what to ask and hope for. The objective of Christ's comfort is exactly that willing spirit: a readiness to pick up, continue the journey, and grow into the Christ-life we share.

It is always tempting to accept false comfort in times of fear and loss: distraction, shallow optimism, codependencies, indulgences. Jesus' warning to the rich—"Woe to you . . . for you have already received your comfort" (Luke 6:24)—applies to any who seek their comfort anywhere but in Christ's strengthening, enlivening, and often demanding companionship. Denial of what we most fear is made easy in a culture that markets distraction and capitalizes on passivity. Leaders who urge us to trust in the military might of the state, preachers who offer Hallmark sermons that skirt around the hard sayings, simplistic therapies that assure us we deserve whatever soothes and numbs our pain forestall the comforts of Christ, who waits in love and infinite patience for us to turn from them to him, though that turning may mean giving up these momentary reliefs.

"I, even I, am he who comforts you," the Lord says in Isaiah (51:12), not to an individual but to a whole people distressed by warfare and the threat of oppression. Don't look for comfort anywhere else. The comfort the prophet proclaims goes well beyond restoration into a vision of liberation and renewal—a new heaven and a new earth: "Shout for joy, O heavens; rejoice, O earth; burst into song, O mountains! For the LORD comforts his people and will have compassion on his afflicted ones" (Isa. 49:13). The assurances elaborated and detailed in ensuing passages of this remarkable book of prophecy are anything but soothing; they are insistent and vigorous reminders of who we are dealing with when we rise out of our sorrows and fears and into the arms of the Almighty:

> Who are you that you fear mortal men,
> the sons of men, who are but grass,

that you forget the LORD your Maker,
   who stretched out the heavens
   and laid the foundations of the earth,
that you live in constant terror every day
   because of the wrath of the oppressor,
   who is bent on destruction?
For where is the wrath of the oppressor?
   The cowering prisoners will soon be set free;
they will not die in their dungeon,
   nor will they lack bread.
For I am the LORD your God,
   who churns up the sea so that its waves
   roar—
   the LORD Almighty is his name.
I have put my words in your mouth
   and covered you with the shadow of my
   hand—
I who set the heavens in place,
   who laid the foundations of the earth,
   and who say to Zion, "You are my people."

Isaiah 51:12–16

Christ, our companion, brings the awesome assurances of this same Creator God to human scale, but it is right to remember that in him the power of the Creator of the Universe resides. "Do not let your hearts be troubled," Jesus tells his disciples. "Trust in God; trust also in me" (John 14:1). It is he whom the winds and the sea obey, and who promises once again, and in new terms, to set prisoners free, feed the hungry, and comfort the widow and the orphan.

He will do it for us and also with us and through us. As members of his body, we are called to comfort and care for one another, to do the work of restoration, and to be agents of real hope to those threatened by fear, self-hatred, or despair. Ours are the hands he extends to the poor, and the eyes that gaze on war-torn flesh and weeping children. "'Comfort ye my people'" saith your God" (Isa. 40:1). It is a word from God to the prophet and to the One who is to come as companion and comforter. It is also a word to us. Being comforted and restored, we are equipped to go and do likewise.

8

CHRIST BENEATH ME

On a memorable day some years ago David Prowse, who played Darth Vader in the original *Star Wars*, visited our daughters' school. An impressive six-foot-five, he scooped up five-year-olds with one hand and held them high above his head at a vertiginous altitude for a small person. I had to catch my breath when my daughter took her turn to be lifted skyward on that large hand, but I also shared the thrill it gave her to feel so securely held at such a height by such a man. Remembering that moment, I think of the Christ who stands beneath us, cheerfully holding us secure, even in what look like precarious places. "Though he stumble, he will not fall," the psalmist writes, "for the Lord upholds him with his hand" (Ps. 37:24). Again and again the psalmist repeats this article of faith: that the Lord "upholds all those who fall and lifts up all who are bowed down" (Ps. 145:14).

He is, as Paul Tillich put it, the "ground of being." When Luther insisted, "Here I stand; I can do no other," the "here" indicated a theological position and a faith commitment, rooted in the promises of the Christ who stood beneath him, offering a secure vantage point from which to survey the world in which his choices were to be made. Christ, as the hymn reminds us, is the solid rock on which we stand. On solid rock we can get our footing. We can find the balance point even when the going is steep and sheer. We can find our "angle of repose," where we can rest secure. What we stand on, literally as well as metaphorically, matters. Reflexologists say all our nerves have terminal points in the soles of our feet. Our feet register information all the time, and transmit it to all parts of the body. They are agents of corporal intelligence that keep us from falling and injuring ourselves. They are also instruments of pleasure, registering the delights of grass, wet sand, deep carpet, polished wood, grainy and gritty footholds in cliff walls.

Rock climbers count on those footholds, and on the belayers who hold them secure as they take what seem to some of us frightening and incomprehensible risks. Typically the belayer comes up from beneath, holding the ropes and gear secure to protect the climber if he or she should fall. The lead climber ventures upward, secured from beneath, open to considerable dangers at times, but investing a good part of his or her confidence in the one who follows below, whose work it is to provide the backup protection in case of a fall. The belayer's is the humbler role but is essential to the whole enterprise. And like a good belayer, the God who humbled himself to serve and support us as we learn feeds us rope and lets us take our risks, holding us secure as we face the dangers that teach us. He sees us from beneath, guarding us as we venture higher and find the way. He knows the way. He is the way. And he can afford to wait for us to find it. He can afford to serve by taking a place beneath us and waiting, who is master of all he sees.

It is no accident that Jesus' model of servanthood took the form of washing the disciples' feet. It was a common practice, but one consigned to the lower social classes. Our language is riddled with notions of the moral order that assigns some persons, things, and actions a "higher"

place than others. What is "beneath" us is worthy of contempt—or at least unworthy of serious attention. So to encounter a Christ, meek and lowly of heart, who takes his place beneath—his hand holding my foot, ready for washing, kneeling or bowing or lying on the earth like the homeless in our parks with "nowhere to lay his head"—is unsettling. Our God language participates heavily in these metaphors of hierarchy: God is "high and lifted up," "above all creation," in the heavens that are "high above the earth." This is as it should be; language like this expresses a fundamental truth about relationship between Creator and creature in terms we readily understand. But every biblical truth is paradoxical, reminding us insistently that God's truth exceeds and confounds human categories. The God who is above all creation not only condescended to take on human form but took on a life of poverty, broke bread with those in the "lowest" social orders, and complicated the complacent religion of the wealthy by identifying with the poorest of the poor. He walked the dusty streets and slept in the wild with "nowhere to lay his head." He embraced the despised and rejected—the street people and the sinners—and became one of them, establishing for all time the ground rule of the divine order: that if we want to find God we must look down, closely and humbly, at what we find "beneath" us. If we are fully to appreciate the truth that God is "above" us, we must also remember the God "beneath" us—humble and complex and necessary and nourishing as the soil.

In his remarkable book about soil—which bears the stark and startling title *Dirt*—William Bryant Logan brings both poetic and scientific understanding to the matter of what lies beneath us as we walk this earth. Humus (the organic matter in topsoil), he reports, is a mystery. "For more than a century," he writes, "chemists have been trying to answer the question, What is humus? And to this date, no one knows. . . . Every time you attempt to break it down into its basic components you get acids of a slightly different nature. . . . In fact, as soil scientist Dr. James Rice puts it, 'It is very possible that no two humus molecules are or have ever been alike.' Like snowflakes or people."[1] What we do know, he concludes, is that the soil, like the humans whose name and bodies come from humus, is "wet, fecund, protean, dangerous."[2] It is life-giving and sustaining, adaptable, humble, and rich with promise. In it all that lives is rooted and grounded. And it is a mystery.

The image of the beloved as "the wind beneath my wings," made popular in the song of that title by Bette Midler, offers an image of sustaining love that coincides with a common notion of what is "spiritual"—a word we've learned to associate with wind and air and light.

It's a good bet that the song would never have gotten off the ground (as it were) if the metaphor had been "the dirt beneath my feet." But God, who is spirit, also became Christ, who was flesh, made from this earth, as we are. Soil is a living substance, an energy source, the stuff from which all life on this planet is made. As embodied beings, we live and move on a delicate layer of topsoil that nurtures all life. We know ourselves, the poet Susan Griffin writes, "to be made from this earth . . . and shaped like the earth, by what has gone before."[3] In a certain sense we might richly and rightly invert the claim that "every good gift . . . is from above" (James 1:17) to acknowledge an equal and opposite truth: that every good gift, on this good earth, comes from below.

The ancient writers knew and valued the soil as the source of all good gifts. "For hardship does not spring from the soil," we read in Job, "nor does trouble sprout from the ground" (5:6). Whatever earthly good we have comes from the earth beneath our feet. If we abuse that earth, we do so not only to the detriment of our physical nourishment but to our spiritual peril. Job compares the erosion of soil to the destruction of hope (14:19), and the comparison is more than metaphor. Those in agricultural societies retain an understanding many of us have largely lost of how God's work begins in the dark and secret places of the earth beneath us. "For as the soil makes the sprout come up and a garden causes seeds to grow, so the Sovereign Lord will make righteousness and praise spring up before all nations," Isaiah writes (61:11). And Mark reminds us, with childlike amazement, "All by itself the soil produces grain—first the stalk, then the head, then the full kernel in the head" (4:28). The soil is the source of goodness and even of virtue; before his rise to power led him astray, Uzziah, the Israelite king, was full of promise, and among his attributes we read that "he loved the soil" (2 Chron. 26:10). Right relationship to the earth is more than a metaphor for right relationship to God. What lies beneath our feet is given to us for divine teaching. When we deplete it or exploit it, we defile it.

Jesus' earthy parables draw our attention repeatedly to the earth and its processes: to the sower scattering seed, to the mingling of wheat and tares, to the long waiting for harvest, to the necessity of hospitable soil. The purpose of parables is to teach us about God. In these stories, God is mirrored in the earth that brings forth life faithfully, renewing it with every turning of the seasons, and we also are called to be bearers of life—good soil, available for cultivation. Christ beneath me upholds and nurtures and renews. He is the context in whom—and on whom—we live and move and have our being.

99

Sometimes, of course, what is beneath us is not solid earth. Sometimes it is the pitching sea that threatens death by drowning. And sometimes God gives us no foothold, but only, it seems, an uncertain ocean on which to float or swim or drift. One of my more memorable dreams has served me for years as a helpful reminder of how God's "upholding" can look dubious and threatening, and what a challenge it is to see with the eyes of faith how we are held securely even in the storm at sea. In the dream I am swimming in the ocean on a brilliant, clear day. The water and the air are exhilarating, and my body feels strong and alive. But suddenly, looking around, I realize there is no land in sight. I begin to panic. *What will I do when I get tired?* I think. Then, in the dream, a voice comes—quite audible and, as I recall, with a hint of amusement: "You know how to swim." This answer only deepens my anxiety. *But what will I do when I get tired?* I ask again. And again the voice comes: "You know how to swim." Again I am unsatisfied, and again I ask. When the voice comes the third time (with more than a hint of amusement) I wake up. The dream has been a gift to me again and again in times of uncertainty, with its assurance that, for now, in the body I've been given, with the life and energy allotted to me, with God's guidance, I have what I need. All we get is manna. And the vast ocean beneath me in the dream is, in fact, a place that upholds me. I float. And I know how to swim. When Christ does not offer himself as "solid rock," he may be offering a different kind of support. On the currents of his vast kindness, "wide, wide as the ocean," I am still upheld. God looked at "the gathered waters he called 'seas,'" we read in the opening chapter of Genesis. "And God saw that it was good" (Gen. 1:10).

There are times we are called upon to swim, or, like Peter, to leap out of the boat and walk on water, though those are mercifully rare. But as earthly creatures, we find our way mostly on land. And Christ is our Way. He offers himself as the path we travel. "You broaden the path beneath me," we read in 2 Samuel, "so that my ankles do not turn" (22:37). Our way is prepared for us. In the Gospels we come to an even richer understanding of the presence of God in Christ, not only as the One who prepares a way but who is the way, and the map, and the lamp unto our feet. We come into a more mysterious and more intimately relational understanding of the One who accompanies and sustains us. A Christian theology of omnipresence takes all God's ways of being "with us always" into account.

One comforting implication of this line from St. Patrick's prayer is built into the language: that the Christ who stands under us understands us. He is our home in this world, which is not our home. On him we find our footing. In

101

the medium of his love we are kept afloat. On the steepest upward way he is ready to catch us if we fall. It is his eyes we meet when we look down into the eyes of a child or of a person squatting in squalor by the side of the road, offering us an opportunity to find him in "the least of these." In him we find our rest at the end of the day, at the end of this life, as we make our final descent, returning our bodies to the earth, and take the final steps of our journey with the One who descended deeper than we will ever have to go to make that journey safe and its completion sure.

9

CHRIST ABOVE ME

"Early in the morning, our song shall rise to thee," we sing in one of the most beloved hymns of the church. And "Jesus comes with clouds descending," in another. And "Angels we have heard on high," every Christmas season, the music tracing the downward path of the angels' descent to the stable. The idea that God, whom the psalmist calls the "Most High," lives "on high" and that Christ ascended into heaven lies at the heart of the story we inhabit. "He sits enthroned above the circle of the earth," Isaiah tells us, "and its people are like grasshoppers. He stretches out the heavens like a canopy, and spreads them out like a tent to live in" (Isa. 40:22).

Even the many who do not cling to the notion that heaven is "up" still find a truth worth reiterating and reflecting on in the language that locates the Lord "above" us.

God is our shade in the desert. He leans over us with compassion and parental solicitude. Like a canopy, his arms encircle us, sheltering us and blessing us with "the blessings of the heavens above" (Gen. 49:25). The God "whose robe is the light, whose canopy space"[1] stretches "above" us from horizon to horizon, carrying us in a wide and steady embrace, even as we struggle like children being held until their rages and wailings abate.

Of course, this language is metaphoric. Locating God is a tricky business. It doesn't take much astronomy for us to realize that our use of terms like "above" and "below" are based on a very earthbound, three-dimensional frame of reference. From a cosmic point of view, the "heavens" are not so much "high above the earth" as encircling and pervading, existing in a dimension beyond the reach of any prepositions. In a series of musings on the facts of contemporary physics, writer David James Duncan offers this bit of bafflement to hierarchical thinkers:

Atomic particles are now believed to derive from immaterial wave packets; space is said to have had ten original dimensions that collapsed, at the beginning of time, to form the superstrings of which subatomic particles consist. Field theory; wave mechanics; morphogenesis; the recently discovered "tunneling" of electrons through neutrons. Through a multitude of images and equations, physics is now telling us that Space, Time, and Matter derive from a source infinitely subtler and greater than all three.[2]

These mysteries are worth pondering, even for those of us with very limited training in the requisite sciences. Indeed, St. Patrick's prayer itself is an invitation to such reflection, its list of prepositions a simple reminder that no one way of thinking about "where" God, or Christ, or the Holy Spirit resides relative to us small, physical, much-loved but much-limited beings is adequate. Awe is an appropriate response to the idea of ten dimensions, or of light years, or of particles that act like waves. Modern physics provides a helpful stay against the literalism that limits the Lord to the dimensions of our imaginations. "For the love of God is broader than the measures of the mind," as an old hymn helpfully reminds us.

In *Out of the Silent Planet*, the first volume of C. S. Lewis's space trilogy, the "higher" orders of creatures exist in a higher frequency—an idea that connects notions of "high" and "low" with density and speed. The "eldila" in this story are creatures barely visible to the human eye, whose bodies seem to be made mostly of light. They are wise folk, a little like angels. In peopling his planet, Lewis plays with the medieval notion of the "Great Chain of Being," inviting us to imagine other creatures quite unlike ourselves who share with us a relationship to God but inhabit the universe on very different terms. The goodness of fantasy fiction lies in this invitation; we need to recognize the limitations of our governing metaphors, including those that limit us to the familiar categories we use to map space and time. Without such acts of imagination, it is easy to fall into the habit of presuming that God sees and acts within comprehensible human categories of high and low, present and past, even good and evil. Much as we need those operating categories, we need frequent and emphatic reminders of God's transcendence to bring us back to humility, wonder, and awe.

Hierarchical thinking will not, however, go away. And it has its uses. The terms *above* and *below* remain meaningful as indicators of status, value, and magnitude. Jesus used them in his final self-disclosures to his still-baffled disciples: "You are from below," he explained in terms they might have some hope of grasping. "I am from above. You are of this world; I am not of this world" (John 8:23). The realm "above" from which he came and to which he returned was the same one the psalmist waved at when he reached the limits of his own imagination in pondering the omnipresence of the Almighty: "Such knowledge is too wonderful for me; it is high, I cannot attain unto it" (Ps. 139:6 KJV).

From Genesis onward, the idea that God occupies a realm "above" all creation pervades the meditations of prayerful people. "Acknowledge and take to heart this day," the writer of Deuteronomy admonishes, "that the LORD is God in heaven above and on the earth below" (4:39). And the psalmist adds, "You have set your glory above the heavens" (Ps. 8:1) and sings "to him who rides the ancient skies above, who thunders with mighty voice" (Ps. 68:33). Some of the greatest liturgical prayers of the church direct our gaze upward, like the ancient "Blessing of the Waters," an Epiphany prayer from the Orthodox tradition:

> The sun sings thy praises;
> The moon glorifies thee;
> The stars supplicate before thee;
> The deeps are afraid at thy presence;
> The fountains are thy servants.
> Thou hast stretched out the heavens like a
>   curtain;
> Thou hast established the earth upon the waters;
> Thou hast walled about the sea with sand.

107

Thou hast poured forth the air that living things
    may breathe.
The angelic powers minister to thee; the choirs
    of archangels worship thee . . .

Prayers like this lovely litany enlarge our vision. Augustine's definition of sin, *"curvatus in se"*—to be "turned in upon oneself"—suggests that the surest correction for sin lies in redirection of our vision, our desires, our hope, our attention to what is outside and beyond the vortex of self-preoccupation.

Years ago, when I was living through a period of deep depression (well before the availability of the current pharmacopoeia of anti-depressant drugs) a friend who had, I'm sure, grown a little tired of my purgatorial circlings around my sorrows, gave me the rather testy but, as it turned out, transformative advice: "Go outside. Look up. The world is bigger than your problems." Despite what I thought at the time was an unnecessarily unsympathetic tone, I took his advice. I went outside and looked up, through the branches of high trees, to the light that suddenly seemed like a constant stream of blessing. I began to sit in my window seat evenings and watch the stars come out. The encircling sky became a refuge. It was the beginning of my journey back to prayer. It was the beginning of a reawakening to James's reassurance that "every good and perfect gift is from above, coming down from the Father of the heavenly lights, who does not change like shifting shadows" (James 1:17).

We look up to get beyond the realm of earthly and earthy transactions and preoccupations, to modify our self-importance, to retrieve a sense of awe at the expanse of the night sky or the sunrise. We look up to remember our own smallness in the scheme of things and set right our perspectives that so easily slip us into a place of primary importance. We look up to be reminded that there are more things in heaven and on earth than are dreamt of in our often self-serving philosophies. And we look up in hope that our gaze is met by One who looks down in love.

Because God did and does look down in love, he "condescended," as the sturdier English of Jacobean England has it, to "usward" (a word a preacher from my childhood used that imparted a certain reassuring image of God hastening in my direction). Condescension gets a bad rap these days; it is hard to find anyone who doesn't bristle at being condescended to. Condescension is patronizing, if not arrogant, undemocratic, uppity, and annoying. Even Jane Austen, who lived in a culture much more accepting of assigned class distinctions than ours (though we tolerate and entrench them more than we like to admit), targeted the condescension of the rich and powerful with well-honed barbs of ironic wit. Only the insipid and obsequious Mr. Collins, whom we are pointedly invited to regard as a fit object of mockery, appreciates the "condescension" of his "patroness," who has looked down from her high social position and taken notice of him. Yet it may be that Mr. Collins has something to teach us about knowing our place. Though the condescension of our privileged fellow citizens may rankle, there is One who descended from a "high" place to meet us on our own turf and our own terms, who laid aside glory and majesty in order (as Eugene Peterson has put it) to "pitch his tent among us" (John 1:14). The appropriate responses on our part are humility and gratitude.

Surely the most disarming image of Christ, even for nonbelievers, is that of the "infant holy, infant lowly" we celebrate every year with hymns that reassert the good news of divine condescension: that "for us men and for our salvation, he came down from heaven."[3] But we could not worship a God who stayed in the manger; the transfiguration, resurrection, and ascension are necessary completions of the story that begins with God's humbling himself into infancy. We need not only know that Christ left a "high place" to come to us, but also that he "ascended into heaven and sitteth on the right hand of God the Father Almighty."[4] Though several key ideas in that claim—ascent, heaven, sitting, right hand, and Father—may carry problematic metaphorical overtones, the truth borne in its very human language remains: Christ is above me, looking down from the high and secure place he left and to which he returned, preparing a place for all of us who await the coming of the "world of love," as Jonathan Edwards called the kingdom of heaven.

In his sermon "The Excellency of Christ," Edwards offers an extended meditation on this point: "There do meet in Jesus Christ infinite highness and infinite condescension." Edwards's focus is that of the entire Reformed tradition, on God's transcendence, on the distance between us and the Holy One who comes to us from a place far higher and a state more mysterious than we can imagine. Clearly and emphatically, then, we cannot begin to bridge that distance, to earn or achieve righteousness, but have to rely on the grace and mercy of a God willing to descend from those heights to come get us—one who seeks and finds and loves us by entering the very dust we are made of and identifying with the poorest and the weakest among us.

Most of us, if we have been blessed with childhoods in which we were cared for and loved, carry deep memories of faces that looked down on us with tenderness, curiosity, kindness, amusement, delight. The parent or grandparent who leaned over us at bedtime, held a sheltering arm around us as we learned to read, looked down from the heights of a sink or desk to watch us play established our foundational sense of security as we began our journeys in this world. It was good to have someone above us, looking down.

The sense of security in knowing someone above me is in charge extends into adult life. I am grateful daily for those who assume administrative duties I would find onerous, those who take on tasks of governance that entail both power and heavy responsibility I'd just as soon not carry (though my gratitude is severely tempered by abuses of power on the part of some in "high places"). I rely on those who willingly invest energy in care of public welfare, care of institutions we count on, supervision (literally the view from above) of the processes by which I receive much of what I need.

Ultimately, all my needs are supplied "from above." The Christ who is above me is prior to me: the head, the firstborn. My three-year-old grandson recently entered a "copying stage": whatever his older brother does, he wants to do in just the same way. Though the boys compete at times, little Matthew's satisfaction comes not from competing and winning but from watching, imitating, following, learning, admiring, and aspiring to what his older brother models. He reminds me how confident and competent one may feel as a subordinate, able to look to those who are "higher" for cues and direction and teaching. I feel this confidence when, in the midst of anxieties about global crises, I can remember that my part is simply to be faithful, not to save the world. Standing above me is someone who sees whole where I see in part, and through a glass darkly.

"Set your hearts on things above, where Christ is seated at the right hand of God," Paul writes (Col. 3:1). Every Sunday, liturgies throughout the world echo this invitation that comes with the force of a command: "Lift up your hearts." As we respond, "We lift them up to the Lord," we may feel even in our bodies a sudden reach upward, a straightening, like a plant turning toward the sun from which it draws nourishment, energy, and direction. We stretch a little beyond our dusty selves and our distractions toward the One who, though unimaginable, our "soul knoweth right well" (Ps. 139:14). We know where to turn. We can find the North Star in the midst of our storms.

Denise Levertov's exquisite poem—one of her last— about Christ's ascension offers one very human vision of what it may have been for him to shed the things of this earth and return to his heavenly state. Not, perhaps, an easy task, even for the glorified Christ:

Can Ascension
   not have been
      arduous, almost
as the return
   from Sheol, and
      back through the tomb
into breath?
   Matter reanimate
      now must relinquish
itself . . .[5]

Relinquishment is the cost of lifting up our hearts. Only letting go, at least momentarily consenting to leave behind the things that bind us to this sticky, earthy life, will lighten us enough to be lifted up into a new plane of encounter with God, awareness of the life of the Spirit, fellowship with the communion of saints, hope of heaven.

10

CHRIST IN QUIET

The "still, small voice" that summoned Elijah from his cave continues to speak (1 Kings 19:12). As the Lord was not in the strong wind or the earthquake or the fire that surrounded the prophet in the wilderness, but in the still, small voice that emerged in their wake, so the same Lord addresses us from an eye of quiet in the midst of the noise and haste we have created—the electronic buzz and flash, the amps and high-decibel drones, the ring tones and the roar of engines—and all the too-much-with-us of contemporary "communication" technologies. For urban and suburban Americans, finding the center of quiet where we can hear the still, small voice is more of a challenge than it has ever been. But it is there, and Christ is waiting in the quiet to meet us.

Much has been written in recent years about the value for all people of faith—not just those in religious orders, and not just Catholics—in reclaiming contemplative practices. Centering prayer, *lectio divina*, and various forms of meditation are regularly featured at spiritual retreats. Those who are willing learn to quiet the mind, pay attention to the inbreath (a gift of new life) and the outbreath (an act of release and relinquishment). They learn to pause where a sentence or word or phrase summons them to reflection. They learn to stay with rather than move on. These apparently simple practices are profoundly countercultural in their resistance to the momentum of habits formed under pressure to produce, to multitask, to stay wired into the vast nervous system the telecommunications industry has fashioned for the body politic.

In response to a hunger that becomes increasingly apparent, forms of these practices have found their way into classrooms and secular sites where clusters of thoughtful people seek periodic relief from the pressures of "getting and spending" and reconnect with their deepest purposes.

The practices range from a few moments of quiet observed at the beginning of meetings or on occasions of common loss to workshops where the language of healing, restoration, and re-creation replace the discourse of achievement, production, and profit. Though we devise new strategies of denial, as well as new ways to address them, our basic needs do not go away. The deepest of these is love. "There is an inner dynamic in the evolution of all true love that leads to a level of communication 'too deep for words,'" writes Thelma Hall in a recent book about *lectio divina*. "There the lover becomes inarticulate, falls silent, and the beloved receives the silence as eloquence."[1] This observation could serve as a fair description of contemplative prayer.

God, who is not limited by any of our notions, can and does speak to us in the words of Scripture and of poetry, in the sounds of nature—even in the thunder and earthquake and fire and hurricane, and in the thundering voices of contemporary prophets. Christ can meet us on the dance floor or in rush-hour traffic. But centuries of testimony by those who have faithfully sought the company of Christ confirm the necessity of quiet to that most intimate encounter. All rules of religious life include times and seasons of silence, acknowledging not only its validity as a mode of healing and hospitality to the God who seeks our company but also the fact that in silence we discover a dimension of the "imitation of Christ," who withdrew repeatedly into the wilderness or the garden to pray in solitude.

Toward the end of his long career as a poet and his circuitous spiritual journey, T. S. Eliot wrote *Four Quartets*, a series of poems that articulate with great complexity and beauty the mystical moments that lift one out of the ordinary and into awareness of divine presence. "At the still point of the turning world, . . . there the dance is," he writes. "Except for the point, the still point, / There would be no dance, and there is only the dance."[2] Dancers know that exhilarating moment of balance, on toe, mid-movement, when what musicians call stop-time occurs in the midst of movement, and a tiny glimpse of timelessness opens up. In the same way, singers and musicians know the power of the pause, the rest, the soundless beat, the silence that reminds listeners of the great embrace of silence in whose circle all music is played. Drumbeats acquire their power from the dialogue of sound and silence. "Words, after speech, reach / into the silence," Eliot reminds us.[3] Language is borne on the outbreath, emerges from and returns to the silence the inbreath requires. The spaces between words, printed or spoken, are dwelling places where something registers

118

and moves inward. When we widen those spaces we open possibility of epiphany.

The sudden knowing, the flashes of clarity we call epiphanies occur in those in-between spaces. In many years of teaching, I have been most delighted by those pregnant pauses in classroom conversation when a student stops mid-sentence because suddenly she "got it." Something "struck" her. What she thought she knew is reframed, not by conscious reasoning but by an insight that seems to come as pure gift. This is the way the Spirit speaks to us. This is how Christ enters the quiet with revelation. In such moments the veil lifts and we are, as Wordsworth put it, "surprised by joy."

Sometimes the testimony to that joy is spontaneous laughter. In a lovely essay on the similarity between poems and jokes, Howard Nemerov focuses on the quality of knowing that comes at that "still point" when expectation gives way to the unexpected and meaning emerges in forms we didn't anticipate. Often, even when the context is nothing we would call comic, we laugh with the sheer pleasure of recognition. The line breaks in modern poems bring us to an edge of anticipation where our expectations are both heightened and, as we move to the next line, often "defeated" and replaced by something slightly unexpected but utterly right. Like jokes, good poems surprise us into seeing differently. And like jokes, they rely on what come-dians know is the prerequisite to all humor: exquisite timing. In the slight pause, the upbeat that precedes the downbeat, a space for a new awareness is created. We miss it if we pass over it too quickly. Quiet only comes with relinquishment of the dubious protections of noise and bustle and "filling" time.

The common notion of "filling" time is curiously at odds with the lovely biblical phrase "the fullness of time" (Gal. 4:4). In that phrase we are reminded how history and providence swell and crest like the waves, and move without our exertions toward ends we have no means to imagine. God works in the quiet mind, when effort ceases and we dwell in the time of germination that is neces-sary for any fruition. "Wait on the Lord," the prophets admonish us. "Be still before the Lord and wait patiently for him" (Ps. 37:7). It is, for some of us, the hardest discipline.

So much of our training is for action. Even our lan-guage makes it hard to imagine silence and inactivity, quiet time, as something that is not "doing nothing." I was amused and edified some time ago to see a sign on the wall of a retreat center admonishing visitors, "Don't just do something—stand there!"

Esau, we read in Genesis 25, became a skillful hunter, but Jacob "was a quiet man, staying among the tents." Though Jacob, like all God's chosen, had his conspicuous imperfections, this detail gives us some clue about those God chooses and uses. Those who are capable of quiet, who withdraw from the mobs and the marketplace to play the lyre and pray in the wilderness, those who seek the silence of the cave and the solitude of the desert make themselves available to the One who comes in quiet and attunes the heart to the subtle ways of the Spirit.

"Don't expand your mind," Melville writes, "subtilize it!"[4] I take him to mean that the intelligence required for spiritual understanding is not that of the argumentative, rational desire for conclusion and closure or for general rules and principles, but a disciplined habit of attentiveness to what might be missed at first glance. When we stop and look closely, slowly, receptively, and quietly, we see the spider spinning its web or the way the slight breeze changes our soundscape. We witness, if we are patient and have the equipment and training, the deep mystery of wave and particle in subatomic space. "Subtle is the Lord," Einstein said, and he had cause to know.[5]

The hardest place to cultivate quiet is in situations of conflict. Our bodies and psyches are programmed for "fight or flight." The impulse to argue seems to emerge almost as early as speech itself. But those who have

121

been trained in nonviolent communication, or bred in pacifist traditions, or schooled in martial arts like aikido, know the power of pausing in the place between fight and flight. They know the skill and trust involved in consenting to the mandate not to "just do something" but to "stand there." Imagine how difficult it must have been for the terrified Israelites, seeing Pharaoh's army approaching behind them, to believe Moses's assurance: "The Lord will fight for you; you need only to be still" (Exod. 14:14).

And yet we have the testimonies of Scripture and all of history that the courage to be still opens a space for the Spirit. The prophet's quiet, as well as his cry, prepares the way of the Lord. All truly prophetic words come out of the depths of the prophetic silences into which God speaks. Because those who live in intimate communion with Christ know what kinds of work can happen only in the quiet places of heart and mind. Listening, for instance. No real listening occurs without laying aside distraction and entering into quiet. "Men listened to me expectantly, waiting in silence for my counsel," Job remembers, recalling the days when "the Almighty was still with me" (Job 29:21, 5). This is not only a nostalgic and wistful longing for days gone by but a recognition of how right relationship is made manifest in voluntary consent to silence before authentic authority.

Only in quiet can we take the rest we need and be restored. Sleep specialists have suggested that those of us who inhabit urban spaces live in the midst of so much ambient noise and light that we neither see nor hear with the acuity that was once possible, because our eyes and ears are so deprived of the darkness and silence they need to repair the wear and tear of daytime use.[6]

Only in quiet can we be released from the tyranny of habit. The reflection required to change our points of view or prejudices necessarily involves stepping off the "moving train," resisting the inertial energy that carries us through so many days from one task to another, and finding a place from which to look at our lives in terms of our deepest sense of calling, in terms of the summoning that draws us toward God, and in terms of the foundational relationship with the Christ who comes to us in mysterious ways and surprises us into awareness. The epiphanic moments that lead to what Eliot called "a shocking valuation of all we have been"[7] are most likely to happen at that "still point" when distractions recede. For some, these moments are matters of regular, daily disciplines of devotion, meditation, and prayer. For some, they are hard-won moments of retreat in the midst of things—the busy mother's short repose during the children's naptime; the teacher's break between classes and preparation when a walk around campus renews the mind; the escape from computer and corporate meeting rooms into an open space for an occasional lunchtime alone. In these times, as Edgar in *King Lear* put it, "ripeness is all." We can open ourselves to the voice of the One who speaks in our silences and receive what we need in even the smallest stretch of available time. But it is up to us to lay aside our agendas for that to happen so that, as the hymn says, "the dear Christ" can "enter in."

In quiet we can encounter Christ on his terms rather than on ours. We easily confuse our busy agendas with God's purposes. As members of a culture that puts a high premium on self-empowerment, we often find it difficult and counterintuitive to rest in uncertainty and openness—to wait, to listen, to accept, to be faithful to the one thing rather than the many. The moments when the Gospels come closest to comedy are those when the disciples (often Peter) conspicuously miss the point of Jesus' instruction and invitation because they can't make the shift from their own habits of mind that involve competition, legalism, scorekeeping, recognition, and measurement to Jesus' way of seeing: paradoxical, countercultural, transcendent, and patient, because he has—and we have—all the time in the world. They miss the point of the transfiguration. They squabble over front-row seats in the kingdom of heaven. They fall asleep in the quiet of Gethsemane. But in the quiet of Easter morning, they begin a new life whose testimonies will all point to what happened in the silence, secret, and darkness of a tomb.

"Be still, and know that I am God," the psalmist writes. "I will be exalted among the nations, I will be exalted in the earth" (Ps. 46:10). The exaltation begins in the quiet when we cease our chatter and clatter, turn from noise and novelty, and, as Mary Oliver beautifully put it, "walk slowly and bow often."[8] Our stillness is an invitation, already accepted by the Christ who stands at the threshold of every quiet space and waits in the depths of the quieting mind for those moments when we make ourselves available. When we are available, the Word is audible.

11

CHRIST IN DANGER

Anyone who frequents airports these days is familiar with the voice on the intercom that reminds passengers that cars or luggage left unattended will be confiscated and that no one is to accept packages from strangers. Posted signs alerted us to the current "threat level." Once, in San Francisco, I recall, it was "blue." I gathered I was to be reassured. In Philadelphia it was "orange"—lower than "red," which means severe, but higher than "yellow," which means elevated. With all this in mind, I duly transferred my three-ounce containers of lotions or liquids into a clear plastic bag and removed my shoes for inspection.

Surely we have much to be thankful for in the many men and women who guard our national and personal security, sometimes putting themselves in harm's way to do so. Still, we know we cannot seal every crack in the system. "Security" may be a reasonable objective, but it may also become a diversion, and even a delusion.

As people of faith we are bound to a particular kind of realism; we know that we live in a fallen world and that God's protection is not necessarily the kind that removes us from real physical danger or from costly consequences. We know this from the daily papers. And we see it in Paul's inventory of the daunting dangers and sufferings he has faced in his travels:

Five times I received from the Jews the forty lashes minus one. Three times I was beaten with rods, once I was stoned, three times I was shipwrecked, I spent a night and a day in the open sea. I have been constantly on the move. I have been in danger from rivers, in danger from bandits, in danger from my own countrymen, in danger from Gentiles; in danger in the city, in danger in the country, in danger at sea; and in danger from false brothers. I have labored and toiled and have often gone without sleep; I have known hunger and thirst and have often gone without food; I have been cold and naked.

Besides everything else, I face daily the pressure of my concern for all the churches. Who is weak, and I do not feel weak? Who is led into sin, and I do not inwardly burn? If I must boast, I will boast of the things that show my weakness.

2 Corinthians 11:24–30

Christ has been with Paul throughout these trials, but the vulnerability, the pain, and the "threat level" have been quite real. And surely the disciples hanging onto halyards and grasping the tiller of the pitching boat where Jesus lay sleeping were under no illusions as to the extent of the danger they faced. It is easy to think Jesus' question—"Where is your faith?"—was a bit unreasonable and unfair. Of course they were afraid! They were sailors. They knew just how close they were to drowning. But the point is that Christ was with them in their danger. He didn't keep them from it but accompanied them in the midst of it. Though he ultimately rose and calmed the storm, and though the narrator concludes the story with the disciples' amazement at his power, the exercise of that power isn't what lies at the heart of the story. The strongest focus is on Jesus' question: "Where is your faith?" In what, in other words, are you investing your sense of security?

I don't believe the point of that question is to suggest that they should, or we should, simply assume that the

Lord will necessarily rush in and snatch us from impending death or damage. I don't believe we are to expect protection from all bodily harm, though many stories of divine protection and reprieve testify to the occasional, exceptional divine intervention. "Where is your faith?" though, is a question that redirects the disciples' attention to a level of security that lies beyond fear of death and beyond death itself. The point of this story might be summed up by Paul's bold assertion that "whether we live or die, we belong to the Lord" (Rom. 14:8).

Do not worry about those who can destroy the body, Jesus tells his disciples in Matthew, but fear those who destroy both body and soul. He does not promise to keep us from disease and death but to hold us safe as we walk whatever dark valleys our journeys take us through. Christ will be with us, as he was with those terrified men in the boat, as he has been with the long lineage of martyrs, as he is with those who live in war zones, as he was with St. Patrick, in every danger. In the storm, in the midst of battle, in the airport under a bomb threat, in the midst of negotiations with volatile governments with nuclear capabilities. He may not prevent what we call disaster, but he will see us through it. He will be in it.

One reason I love the prayer of St. Patrick is the way its litany of prepositions calls us to reflect on the nature of our relationship with Christ: how it is that he is with us, behind us, before us, above us, beneath us. When we come to the line "Christ in danger," several meanings seem possible.

The most obvious is that Christ is with us when we are in danger. He accompanies, he witnesses, he protects, he sees us through. There will be dangers, there will be real risk, there will be real loss. And Christ will be with us as we suffer what we must and learn what we can from those circumstances. But a second dimension of that affirmation is that Christ is also "in danger." Christ shared all our human vulnerabilities, even unto death by torture. And where is he now? In the cells of those being tortured. And in the villages where Sudanese or Rwandan or Ugandan children are being abducted. And with victims of human trafficking. What is being done to the least of these is being done to him. The dangers sustained by the body of Christ throughout the world are dangers sustained by Christ, who lives still, sacrificially and sacramentally, in our midst. When we put one another in harm's way, when we threaten one another with retaliation or retribution or revenge, we put Christ in the danger he chooses to share with us. We do it to the least of these and we do it to him.

131

A third way of reading this line also seems worth mention, though it may be the most counterintuitive: Christ is at work in the danger itself. God, who acts in mysterious, sometimes baffling, sometimes frustrating ways, may summon us to faith precisely in situations of danger. Stories of the lives of saints abound in which a quantum leap of faith occurs in the midst of danger. Facing the roaring lion, being led to the stake, left in a prison cell, or nailed to a cross, they would be given a sudden clarity, calm, or courage. They had what they needed. Some prayed for their persecutors. Some sang. Some raised their eyes to heaven in unlikely silence. What came to them in the danger appears to have been a gift of faith enlarged by crisis, tried in fire that turned it to gold.

We live in dangerous times. Though this statement has always been true, the particular dangers we face as a people and as a species are of historically unprecedented magnitude. So our witness as people of faith needs to include a full reckoning both of the dangers that threaten us and of the dangers we impose on others by the way we choose to live—dangers to the poor, to the planet, to those who suffer from unjust policies. It is certainly our responsibility to mitigate those dangers where we can, to seek and offer practical protection, and to consider what we endanger by poor stewardship of power and resources.

As we seek human solutions to human problems, Jesus' question "Where is your faith?" remains as pertinent and urgent for us as it was for the disciples in the pitching boat. In what do we invest our sense of security? What reassurances do we grasp at? What are we willing to do to protect ourselves from death, from deprivation, or even from inconvenience? How does misplaced faith actually put others in danger? And where do we look for help when we are the vulnerable ones?

Seeking to protect ourselves may make us cruel. Pursuing our own security may make us blind to others' welfare. Investing our faith in anything but the One who is, as the catechism reminds us, "our only hope in life and death" leads us into spiritual danger much more consequential than the threats we may so easily be made to fear.

I'm not sure I fully agree with Franklin Roosevelt's bold claim that "the only thing we have to fear is fear itself," but it has some merit in light of repeated biblical admonitions to "fear not." Fear not, for I am with you. I am with you always. Perhaps fear is the danger against which Christ offers his surest protection—more than danger to life and limb, abject fear can destroy the confidence, the trust, and the lively, loving alertness to the opportunities of the moment that characterize a life lived fully in faith. The disciples' fear in the boat gives us a measure of faith in that, as the story makes clear, they hadn't yet made the paradigm shift into a larger understanding of the unfolding story of salvation—a story to whose climactic moments they were still unwitting witnesses.

A woman I know who survived two Polish concentration camps as a child told me once of a moment of psychological and spiritual liberation she experienced when she fully faced her own death. "When you are not afraid of death anymore," she said simply, "you are free." Getting beyond fear of death is no simple matter; we're wired for self-protection and survival. But Jesus invites us to venture beyond that fear and into a larger realm of confidence that comes only when we recognize the reassuring presence of Christ in the very eye of the dangers we face—personal and global.

The lesson behind Jesus' rebuke to the disciples at sea—and I believe it was a gentle rebuke, full of compassion for the ones he called "my little children"—is that perfect love casts out fear. That beyond the cloud of fear lie freedom, confidence, and empowerment beyond what most of us dare to imagine. There are fearsome things in this world. There is darkness. There are threats—way up in the red zone. There is danger. And Christ is in it with us. Always. Even unto the end of the world.

12

CHRIST IN HEARTS OF
ALL THAT LOVE ME

Love has a thousand faces, to paraphrase Virginia Woolf.[1] Some of those faces, I might add, are exceeding strange. Hardly a family exists in which an eccentric relative or quirky sibling doesn't arise to complicate the terms on which we consent to love those given to us to love. My grandfather, for instance, who I'm quite sure loved my brother and me, also loved sundry neighborhood children enough to give them our toys, and on one occasion, our puppy. My brother, who, as we grew up together, loved me in his own misguided way, practiced wrestling holds on me without benefit of permission and taught me everything from chess to tennis for the express purpose, it seemed, of having someone he could mercilessly and consistently beat. Parental love, kind and gentle as it was, came from people who got no rehearsal time and found their way in child-raising as their parents did with them, relying on whatever curious mix of culture, community, common sense, and prayer was available. We love one another recklessly, joyfully, selfishly, ignorantly, sacrificially, desperately—often expecting the wrong things, jealously guarding what needs to be liberated, running dry because the roots of our love have not reached deeply enough into the life source that is the heart of God. Still, in all our imperfections, seeing one another "through a glass, darkly," or as shadows cast on the wall of Plato's cave, our capacity to love one another is where we most clearly reflect the image of God.

One of the best known of the beautiful chants from Taizé repeats the simple claim, "*Ubi caritas et amor, Deus ibi est*"—where there is love, there is God. God is love. It doesn't get any simpler than that, or any more mysterious. The sum of all the law and the commandments is to love God with our whole heart and soul and mind and strength, and our neighbors as ourselves. All true spiritual seeking leads us to love—but for most of us, that seeking leads us along bumpy and circuitous paths of relationship where we encounter love in unfamiliar and often unsettling guises. Sometimes the challenge of Christ's commandment to love one another lies not so much in extending love to others but in accepting others' love, tainted and imperfect as our own, as it is offered. It can be hard to accept that Christ's own love is being channeled to us through the demands of a small child or the oversight of a managerial colleague or the unwelcome attentions of a tiresome and needy acquaintance. It can be hard to remember that we're all here on the same assignment—to learn to love one another and God—and that we are given one another to practice on. But if Christ is "in hearts of all who love me," I have to be prepared to seek, find, and accept his invitation to recognize him in the particular folk who, after their various fashions, and surprisingly, love me. Most of them do not live in monasteries or devote their days to the practice of prayer. Most of them are caught in webs of cultural confusions and pressures, as I am, and have to keep remembering to breathe. Our love of one another is fragmented and faulty, but it is where the love of Christ is made most visible and accessible.

Wendell Berry, whose fiction offers memorable images of "the beloved community," has provided contemporary readers with images of Christlike love as luminous and useful as any in contemporary story. In his wonderful tale "Fidelity," Wendell Berry contrasts the sterile, impersonal, technology-ridden caregiving of a modern hospital with the care of friends and relatives who visit a dying man, representing, in their inexpert simplicity, "the larger, looser, darker order of merely human love."[2] They stand at his bedside, uncertain about his condition and unqualified to make detailed medical decisions but clear about what he needs and has always needed from them. They want him to die among them as he has lived among them, encircled by a loving community who knows him by name and who can see him through his last passage with appropriate attention and hope that is true and transcendent rather than the false hope of physical recovery.

Without the sentimentality that reduces love of family and friends to the dimensions of a greeting card, Berry invites us to imagine what love looks like when it is lived out faithfully among people who know themselves to be dependent on the same soil and seasons, and accountable to one another. The descriptors "large" and "loose" and "dark" suggest characteristics of human love we do well to remember and value: the best of human love is inclusive; it grows over time and takes in new people; it flourishes in the midst of sorrow and survives against the odds even when it is disappointed or violated. It is not indestructible—only God's love is—but it can be unconditional, and where it is rooted in love of God, it is radical and resilient. As embodied beings, we need love in the flesh, and so we got the incarnation, and so we get the Christ-gift in each other, like flecks of real gold that show up in the most ordinary pebbles.

The ways of human love are as various as the courses of streams, each one leading to the ocean. I think of my grandmother who read me the same story a hundred times just because I wanted to hear it again; of my father, whom I found eccentric and embarrassing but whose lively stories have become a legacy I cherish; of a friend who never let me get away with sloppy tennis; another who encouraged me to break a few unnecessary rules; another who raised my political awareness in a dark and painful moment of personal and national history; and another who evoked, and cherished, my laughter. Some have been there for a short season, some for a longer shared journey. Longevity is not the test of authentic love, but rather what gifts are exchanged, and in what spirit. I remember a few passing conversations with near strangers that left indelible marks on my memory, signatures of human love freely offered.

In his now classic work *The Four Loves*, C. S. Lewis offers rich reflections on each kind of human love and its particular relationship to divine love: affection, friendship, eros, and charity. Affection (an English term he deems closest to the Greek *storge*) is, in effect, the love that "comes with the territory"—the natural inclination toward those given to us in family and home community whom we did not choose but among whom we work out the terms of our lives. Under "normal" or healthy circumstances, we don't have to work to attain this love, or to feel it; we grow into it and receive it as naturally as we receive other gifts of the environment we call our own. "Home," my father used to say with a slightly wry smile, "is where, when you go there, they have to let you in." They have to because they love you, and the love, ragged and worn as it may be, is pure gift. Christ comes to us in those hearts as one who is simply given—not earned, not studied, not even chosen, just available and ours to receive.

Friendship (*philia*), the second of the four loves Lewis identifies, rests on common tastes and interests and desires. We find our way into shared endeavors with those whose hopes and inclinations mirror our own. Or we recognize even in someone very different a fitting

140

complement, a person we can trust to tell us the truth, a teacher from whom we can learn some of the life lessons we need. Christ comes to us in the hearts of friends who return our badly placed serves, critique our facile conclusions, challenge our opinions, forgive our follies, encourage our efforts to grow, and show up in the midst of humiliation or confusion or mourning, offering a ministry of presence that needs few words. In the hearts of friends, Christ comes to us, reminding us that we are sought and chosen and valued in all our particulars.

The love called "*eros*," a term we import from the Greek partly to retain its complexity and distinguish it from oversimplified versions of romantic or sexual love so pervasive in popular culture, brings the charge of heightened, specific desire and devotion. Dangerous it may be—certainly Lewis finds it so—but erotic love in its largest sense can lift up our hearts to a place of self-sacrifice and generosity unlike any other. In those who love us this way, Christ comes to us as the "tremendous lover," or the bridegroom of biblical poetry and parable who seeks us as his own. Courtship and marriage at their best teach us irreducible lessons about the love that came to find us, paid the ultimate cost, and went ahead to prepare a wedding banquet and make a home for us.

The love Lewis identifies as the most wholly Christlike, charity or *agape*, is the love most like God's self-giving love. This is the love we are called to and challenged to learn. Unconditional, not dependent on reciprocity or even recognition, overflowing from a God-source that "makes the desert to flourish," it manifests most accurately and fully the love of Christ, and of a Creator God who made us to become companions and friends. It is this love, with its roots deep in the love of God, that enables us to pause and see and speak to a street person, or work tenderly with those convicted of violent crimes, or spend precious hours of our own lives with the mentally handicapped or even with the bores and the boors and the self-absorbed. Lewis says of God's charitable love, "He is so full, in fact, that it overflows, and He can't help but love us."[3] Such love is joyful, regardless of return, and rich with life. We may call it a virtue. It is an attribute of God, and we are capable of it only to the extent that we consent to be channels of what we did not earn or invent or even cultivate. In the hearts of those who love us this way, we come as close as this life lets us to seeing Christ face to face.

Those who did see Christ face to face received and inscribed for the rest of us the commandment that lies at the heart of our life together as the body of Christ: "A new command I give you: Love one another. As I have loved you, so you must love one another" (John 13:34). Believing in and obeying that command, we begin the process of becoming Christ-bearers, channels of love, channels of peace, instruments of God's action in the world. As God uses human hands to minister to the needs of others, preparing food, repairing shelters, wielding tools and human tongues to deliver messages of hope and liberation and, at times, the prophetic word into a faithless world, so God also uses human hearts to love—actively, creatively, specifically, faithfully—trusting, hoping, and persevering. It is a large assignment—enough for a lifetime of practice. There is no end to learning how to love; every encounter offers us a new occasion for that learning.

We learn to love in very human, complex, troubling relational and political contexts. The command given in Deuteronomy, for instance, comes to us over the centuries with renewed force as we wrestle with immigration issues: "And you are to love those who are aliens, for you yourselves were aliens in Egypt" (Deut. 10:19). The story of the Good Samaritan teaches us a rich and challenging answer to the question "Who is my neighbor?" and breaks open the embrace that tends to close around immediate family and close friends. "Love your enemies" is arguably the most difficult and challenging command of all Jesus issued. As we've never done it very well, a fact every war demonstrates, it keeps us at our learning edge. The Christ who dwells in the hearts of all who love me also reaches across great divides every time someone dares to love me although I am, and my people are, the enemy.

"Now that you have purified yourselves by obeying the truth," Peter writes, "so that you have sincere love for your brothers, love one another deeply, from the heart" (1 Peter 1:22). Obedience, preceded by faith, precedes, trains, and deepens love. Though Christ can and does use broken, and what Jeremiah called "desperately wicked," hearts as instruments of love, the greatest blessing of human love comes to us when, like water that has been filtered and purified, or that comes fresh from an unpolluted stream, it comes as a by-product of loving God first. "Dear friends," writes John, whose Gospel perhaps most luminously shows us what love looks like, "let us love one another, for love comes from God. Everyone who loves has been born of God and knows God" (1 John 4:7). This generous, inclusive word acknowledges all authentic human love, whatever love survives in even the most corrupted heart, as a gift of God. "No one has ever seen God," John goes on, "but if we love one another, God lives in us and his love is made complete in us" (1 John 4:12). Our job is to love. God's is to begin this process and to make that love complete, to perfect it, to make good, as it were, the debt we owe to one another and to the One who made us and holds us and waits for us with infinite patience. In the meantime, which is where we live, what we have to work with is each other. God works in the very people who challenge and limit and correct me, who irritate and delight and surprise me. They are the ones through whose hearts the love of Christ is reflected and refracted, bent and broken into a prism of possibilities, warming my own heart and keeping it open.

13

Christ in Mouth of Friend and Stranger

Moses, called by God to speak, responded the way many of us would: "O Lord, I have never been eloquent. . . . I am slow of speech and tongue. . . . please send someone else to do it." The Lord's answer is a good reminder to the rest of us—the hesitant, the fearful, and the lazy: "Who gave man his mouth? . . .

147

Now go; I will help you speak and will teach you what to say." When Moses still demurs, God offers him Aaron as a spokesman, though not as a substitute, and being God and much more patient with his reluctant servants than we might be, he adds a promise: "I will help both of you speak and will teach you what to do. He will speak to the people for you, and it will be as if he were your mouth and as if you were God to him" (excerpts from Exod. 4:10–16).

Moses was an odd pick. He evidently had a speech impediment, or at least suffered from a strong resistance to public speaking. But God made him spokesperson to the people of Israel. Again and again, God chooses unlikely agents—prophets, preachers, teachers—to carry his messages. One clear conclusion we may draw from the many stories of God's choosing is that the word of God can and will come to us in strange people and surprising ways.

The prophets and poets of the Old Testament and the apostles of the New Testament have this in common: they are ordinary, flawed people. And God put words in their mouths. "Then the LORD reached out his hand," Jeremiah writes, "and touched my mouth and said to me, 'Now, I have put my words in your mouth'" (Jer. 1:9). Daniel gives a similar testimony: "Then one who looked like a man touched my lips, and I opened my mouth and began to speak" (Dan. 10:16). Like them, Isaiah attributes his words to God: "I have put my words in your mouth and covered you with the shadow of my hand" (Isa. 51:16). And the psalmist recognizes God as the source of his own praises: "He put a new song in my mouth, a hymn of praise to our God" (Ps. 40:3).

There are still those who, like the prophets, officially and recognizably speak for God—preachers and prophets in our time, leaders in faith to whom we look for guidance. False prophets also abound, of course, and, ironically, one of the marks of inauthenticity is the often strident public insistence that one's own point of view is also God's. But the truth remains that God works through ordinary, unqualified, often unsuspecting people. Precisely the word we need may be brought to us in ordinary encounters—with friend or stranger. Knowing that, we listen for God's guidance, expecting surprise. It may come from one of the "strangers" we take in—one of the least of these who is to be received as Christ. It may be that a chance encounter is a divine encounter. We must allow for that possibility.

So we need to listen, in private conversation and in public transactions, in a spirit of discernment and in conversation with our brothers and sisters in faith. We need the correctives and challenges of an interpretive community and of Scripture itself, plumbed and pondered, so as not to be gullible and led astray, or, on the other hand, so as not to become so critical that we miss the corrective word. This is why "the priesthood of all believers" is such an important principle in Reformed tradition; we are all, as a community of people, listening for God, called to be attentive, expectant, and discerning in our listening and speaking. "Christ be in my ears and in my hearing," an old prayer reads: in all my listening, let me be attuned to the voice of Christ, who may speak in mouth of friend and stranger.[1]

This is part of what it means to pray without ceasing: to listen for God—in ordinary encounters, to listen for the word we need to hear, the invitation, the correction, even though the person through whom it comes may be quite unaware that he or she is serving as a messenger. Listening for God is the ground of obedience. The word *obey* comes from a Latin word that means to listen. In listening for the voice of Christ, we obey his call.

Some time ago I felt moved to visit an Al-Anon meeting out of concern for a close friend struggling with alcoholism. The meeting was both helpful and humbling. The common commitment to the healing process outlined in the twelve-step program was reviewed at the outset. Then those who wished to were invited to speak about their own lives and concerns, briefly, and with no "cross-talk," as they put it. Each speaker shared his or her story as a free gift to others, not knowing whether or in what way it might be useful.

As it happened, the first three people to speak addressed quite directly the situation and anxieties that were on my heart. I had come asking for guidance and help, hoping to discern my own role in a difficult situation. I was given that help. Those who gave it didn't know me, but Christ was there "in mouth of friend and stranger," and, I believe, in my ears and in my hearing. I went away blessed.

In Quaker meetings I attended for several years, I often had a similar experience of direct address and of specific answers to prayers for guidance or insight that came from individuals who rose and spoke what was on their hearts with no notion of what particular needs their words might be meeting. Their words were freely offered and gratefully received, independent of their own intentions.

In twelve-step meetings, Quaker meetings, therapy groups, prayer groups, and other intentional gatherings, this kind of speaking and listening often provides answers to prayer and timely directives. Speaking and listening in such settings offers us a deeper understanding of how words work as a currency of grace, as does the practice of *lectio divina*, where we read Scripture listening

151

for the word or phrase that addresses us directly and pertinently.

But in the clatter of ordinary life outside those protected and sacred spaces, it is more difficult to listen with that same quality of attention. It is difficult because the demands on our attention are legion, insistent, and noisy. We live with interruptions, intrusions from marketers, and all manner of dispensable drivel. Simply in order to stay focused, there may be much we have to handle with dispatch, or dismiss.

So how do we listen for God as we walk through the noise and haste? How do we listen for Christ in mouth of friend and stranger when so many of the words we hear come to us courtesy of commercial media? Or one end of a too-public cell phone conversation? Or the rote responses of a tired person behind a counter? Or the taped message from the insurance company that our call is very important to them?

Here's what we can do. We can carry with us the question, "How may God be addressing me in this encounter?" How, for instance, am I being invited to slow down? To reflect? To reconsider? To open up some new avenue of thought or feeling? To widen my embrace or reexamine my reasoning? To confront? We can at least consider Carl Jung's assertion that all interruptions are divine messages. (Though I'd be a little skeptical of accepting that claim without qualification, considering the manifold electronically mediated interruptions that have become the background noise of contemporary life!) We are given to each other as teachers. The encouragements and the criticisms, the affirmations and the irritations alike may be gifts from God.

Jesus promised the disciples that words would be given them as they ventured forth on their ministries, sure to face persecution. "Do not be anxious how you are to speak or what you are to say," he told them, "for what you are to say will be given to you in that hour. For it is not you who speak, but the Spirit of your Father speaking through you" (Matt. 10:19–20). Like the manna that came to the Israelites through no merit or work of their own, God may give us words when they are needful, in ways that do not depend on any particular wisdom we may think we have to impart. Paul, writing to the Ephesians, understands this dependency on the Holy Spirit as the only reliable source of wisdom and right speaking: "Pray also for me, that whenever I open my mouth, words may be given me so that I will fearlessly make known the mystery of the gospel" (Eph. 6:19).

The important thing about both Jesus' assurance and Paul's appeal is the emphasis on divine provision and intention. It is our part to take care in what we say, to cultivate precision and discretion, and not to be too quick to impose our homemade, humanly made opinions. But as Christ-bearers, as friends and strangers, it is good to know that God may use our words in ways we do not foresee and do not need to control. Christ may speak through me if I am simply willing, praying, like Paul, to be given words that will be a gift to someone.

Every teacher I know has been surprised on occasion by what students remember. We think we know what they need to learn, and we organize our lectures accordingly. But the most significant moments of learning often occur by dint of an offhand remark, a by-the-way illustration, a word choice or an image we had no idea would be of more than incidental importance. If we pray that Christ be in our mouths and in our speaking, we can trust that he will use our words in ways we cannot anticipate—for healing, for understanding, for comfort.

We have no way of knowing for sure when our words are working to that effect, and that is as it should be. It would be foolish to assume that once we've prayed to be used, our every utterance becomes a pearl of divine wisdom. But God does use us and other unlikely proxies in his own time and in unexpected ways. Whether we speak or listen, we do the work of God when we consent to be his instruments and leave the results up to him.

Though in his sovereignty, God can act without even that much collaboration, he invites our participation, as speakers and listeners in the work of the kingdom.

When I was nineteen, a word from a complete stranger kept me from what might have been a self-indulgent and self-destructive decision when she saw me light what she had no way of knowing was my very first cigarette. She hesitated briefly, then came over to me and said very gently, "I know it's not exactly my business, but I just want you to know how much harm a habit like that can do you. I hate to see a beautiful young person like you smoking." She said this with lightness of tone and kindness in her eyes. She told me briefly about her own daughter's struggle to quit smoking. I put out my inaugural cigarette, and that was the end of that particular bad habit, stopped by a good word in the mouth of a stranger. Encounters like that make me wonder about the wisdom of minding our own business. Certainly that ethic has to be balanced with caring for one another and being open to speaking, caringly and with discernment, what God puts on our hearts, the words he puts in our mouths.

Kindly advice or timely observations from friendly folk may not be too hard to accept as agents of grace. What can be harder is the word that comes from an alien or enemy. Think how hard it is to listen attentively for what God might be offering in the words of a person at the other political extreme—or the person you know to be at complete odds with you on a particularly divisive issue. Or the person who has hurt you.

We need sometimes to protect ourselves from harsh words, and we need to have our disagreements honestly and even vigorously; it is part of how we work things out. But to be open to the idea that someone you find insufferably wrong-headed might still bear you a gift, and to ask God to bless your listening in encounters with them, might be to open a path for grace and reconciliation.

Intentional listening of this kind can be a source of pleasure. The intent to glean a gift can transform a conversation from a sterile exercise in endurance to a practice of enlivening curiosity. I had a chance to practice this just this past week as I sat by my speakerphone waiting (twenty-five minutes, as it turned out) for the voice of a human being while hearing the repeated recorded message that my call was very important to the insurance company. The human being who eventually came to the phone was not a petty bureaucrat mouthing language from the professional manual but a kindly and sympathetic soul who, for ten minutes, became my teacher. I emerged from a trying and confusing insurance snafu simply grateful that there were people willing to shuffle the paper and track the numbers necessary to pay for my mother's health care. Theirs is patient—sometimes heroically patient—work, as far as I can tell, and some of those strangers at the other end of a long telephone tree are out there being agents of grace. This is not, by the way, my usual attitude, lest you imagine I have a gift of unusual patience. But the line from St. Patrick's prayer helped me. The fact that I had been meditating on Christ in mouth of friend and stranger made a significant difference, in this instance, in what I was able to hear.

Think how often in the Gospels a word of truth comes from an unlikely source—from the stranger or even the enemy: the Samaritan (hated enemy of pious Jews), the adulterous woman, the tax collector who collaborated with the despised Roman government, even the demons who recognized and named Jesus as the Christ before any of his disciples—these and other characters in Gospel stories remind us that anyone among us, friend or stranger, may be an agent of grace and a teacher. Isn't it startling that it is the demons, and Pilate, who rightly identify Christ when the disciples still don't get who he is? Sometimes our enemies know something we need to know. They may simply bring us an occasion for learning how to reach beyond our customary assumptions and habits and imagine our way into another person's or tribe's story.

We can learn from political adversaries, even as we confront them vigorously. Or from the gang member who consents to an interview, even as we seek to protect young people from the gang he represents. Or from the addict who has been humbled and offers her story of healing. Or from the fellow Christian who reads the same passage we read in a different way. Occasions for divine encounter abound in the most ordinary and familiar sites of daily life. Despite much speaking that is not of God, we can learn to attune ourselves in prayer to listen, as one writer put it, "through the noise to the music"—to listen for the voice of Christ, asking, "Is it you, Lord?" and saying, with Samuel, who heard a voice in the night, "Speak, Lord, your servant is listening."

God awaits us everywhere. Christ accompanies us. The Holy Spirit puts words in mouths of friend and stranger. This is the point of St. Patrick's prayer, rich with prepositions that remind us not to locate God in some remote heaven of our imaginations but to live in the presence of a God who is both hidden and manifest, moving among us, who seeks us out and speaks to us in surprising ways. If we listen with willing hearts, we will hear him.

Questions for Reflection

1. Christ Be With Me

1. How and when have I most vividly experienced Christ's presence with me?
2. How do I understand Jesus' promise, "I am with you always, even unto the end of the age"?
3. How does John's statement that "God is light" deepen my understanding of God's ways of being present to us? What is to be learned by linking that image to my experience of natural light?
4. What human experiences of being stayed with or accompanied evoke most clearly my sense of loving companionship? When has a person offered me a

"ministry of presence" that imparted Christ's peace or healing?

2. Christ Within Me

1. What practices have helped me "listen inward" for the promptings of the Holy Spirit who works through our truest intuitions, impulses, desires?
2. What might it mean to practice more regularly the awareness that I am a "Christ-bearer"?
3. How does receiving the Lord's Supper help me foster this awareness?
4. What makes most vivid and real to me the fact that God dwells immanently in the created order that he made and loves?
5. How might I benefit from remembering regularly the Quaker saying that "there is that of God in everyone"?

3. Christ Behind Me

1. In what particular ways do I need Christ to be "behind me"? How does that image define some of the kinds of help I need?

2. When have I been most effectively coached from the sidelines, urged on by a supporter, or "backed up" by team members? What are my best experiences of help coming from behind?

3. How may the image of "Christ behind me" help me reflect on the wisdom and kindness of consenting at times to be the follower, the one who walks behind or stays after?

4. Thinking of the woman who approached Jesus from behind seeking healing, whom might I encounter if I turned and took a longer look at those ("the least of these") whom I walk past, hurried and preoccupied?

4. Christ Before Me

1. When have I been most aware, at least in retrospect, that Christ, going before me, prepared the way for what needed to happen? What have those experiences taught me about hope and expectation?

2. How and when am I aware of feeling "led" to act? What kind of help do I need in discerning the difference between my own inclinations and the leadings of the Holy Spirit?

3. What if, for a time, I substituted "follower of Jesus" for my customary uses of the term "Christian"? How

161

might that change my sense of what I am about in my daily spiritual walk?

4. When does Christ simply stand before me, summoning me into encounter? When has an image or a person stopped me and startled me into awareness of the Christ who faces me with a direct, loving, compassionate, and questioning gaze?

5. Christ Beside Me

1. How does the image of Christ walking "beside" me awaken a different response from the image of the Christ who walks behind or before? What does it help me to imagine and understand about the ways he accompanies us?

2. In what practical ways might I "come alongside" others in need? How can I live out that call to the ministry of companionship?

3. How might I recognize the presence and call of Christ in the one who is "beside me" in marriage, at work, at table, on the road?

4. How might I change my physical location periodically—in worship, at work, in line, on the plane, at gatherings—to become more aware of those I live among and share life's resources with? To whose side do I tend to gravitate? At

whose side might I find myself in new kinds of conversation?

6. Christ to Win Me

1. What do I need to be won away from? What am I clinging to?
2. To what do I need to be won over? Where am I still resistant, hesitant, untrusting, uncertain?
3. How do the human situations of battle and courtship respectively suggest ways to reflect on the self-sacrificial love of a God who seeks to "win" me?
4. How, as I look back, can I see my story as a story of grace unfolding, often without my own efforts or awareness?

7. Christ to Comfort and Restore Me

1. What kind of comfort do I need? What are the parts of my daily living that leave me needing comfort?
2. Where do I tend to seek false comforts? What do they assuage? How might I shift my dependencies to Christ as the source of comfort?

3. What, in my life, needs restoration? To what do I need to be restored? How might restoration come about?

4. How can I learn to be a bearer of Christ's comfort? Who has been that for me?

8. Christ Beneath Me

1. What is helpful to me in images of Christ as the "ground" or "rock" on which I stand?

2. How might the image of Christ "beneath me" help make us more acutely aware of the ways the earth itself, the soil, the water, support and nourish us?

3. How may a life of faith require that we learn to "float"?

4. If I were able to imagine and believe that Christ really stands ready to catch me if I fall, what might I be willing to attempt?

9. Christ Above Me

1. Knowing what we do about the limitations of the metaphorical language that locates God and heaven as "up," how does the metaphor still serve important purposes for the Christian imagination?

2. How might an understanding of some of the post-Einstein ideas of time and space help to open up and modify whatever limitations there may be in thinking of heaven as "up" and earth as "down"? How can we bring what we know from the sciences to bear upon our practical theology?

3. In my experience of life in family, church, and workplace, how do hierarchical thinking and hierarchical structures help? How do they become problematic?

4. What is helpful about Augustine's definition of sin as being "turned in upon oneself"?

10. Christ in Quiet

1. Where are the quiet spots in my day and life? What happens in quiet that can't happen for me elsewhere?

2. How do I use music, talk radio, television, telephone, and other sources of noise? Where might I be using them to avoid the challenge of the quiet that allows room for God to speak?

3. What practices have helped me learn to quiet my mind and the inner noises my mind generates as distractions?

4. In what circumstances might I need to practice "being" rather than "doing"?

11. Christ in Danger

1. In what do I invest my sense of security?
2. In the midst of the actual and potential dangers we live with now, how might I deepen my sense of ultimate safety?
3. How might we apply the idea of Christ as present in "the least of these" to those who are most vulnerable and endangered by poverty, war, or the contaminations and polluting practices that lead to disease? How might focusing on those who live in those particular dangers help us to recognize new dimensions in our calling as followers of Christ?
4. How might an awareness of the terms and consequences of our war-making, weapons manufacture, and economic policies help me focus my energies rightly—on reducing danger where it is possible, and learning how to face it where it is inevitable?

12. Christ in Hearts of All That Love Me

1. How have those who love me expanded and diversified my understanding of what love looks like?
2. Where have I experienced love that is hard—"tough love"—that has helped and trained me? What have I learned about giving that kind of love?

3. What have been some of my confusions about human and divine love? What kinds of distortions and oversimplifications seem important to recognize and reject in learning how to love and be loved?

4. What opens up if we approach "Who is my neighbor?" as a political question?

13. Christ in Mouth of Friend and Stranger

1. When has a word from a stranger come as a gift of timely help or direction?

2. Whose words might I be inclined to dismiss? Where might I listen with a more open mind or heart?

3. What does it mean to be a good listener? To whom do I go for that gift? What might I learn from them?

4. What might I need to learn about discerning when to speak and when to keep silent?

Notes

Introduction

1. Commonly attributed to St. Augustine.

Chapter 1: Christ Be With Me

1. Emily Dickinson, "Poem 1129," *The Complete Poems of Emily Dickinson*, ed. Thomas H. Johnson (Boston: Little, Brown & Co., 1960), 506.

2. Gerard Manley Hopkins, "God's Grandeur," *Gerard Manley Hopkins: A Selection of His Poems and Prose* (New York: Penguin Books, 1954), 27.

3. Elie Wiesel, quoted in Harry James Cargas, *Harry James Cargas in Conversation with Elie Wiesel* (New York: Paulist Press, 1976), 94.

Chapter 2: Christ Within Me

1. Karl Barth, *Church Dogmatics* I/2; II/2 (Edinburgh: T. and T. Clark, 2007), 240, 117.

2. Mother Teresa of Calcutta in interview with Dan Rather, CBS. Recounted by Bob and Debby Gass, *Word for Today*, Winter 2006/7 (entry for Friday, November 3, 2006).

Chapter 4: Christ Before Me

1. T. S. Eliot, "Burnt Norton," *Four Quartets* (New York: Harcourt, Brace, Jovanovich, 1943, 1971), 19.

Chapter 5: Christ Beside Me

1. Francis Thompson, "The Hound of Heaven," *Sacrifice of Praise*, ed. James H. Trott (Nashville: Cumberland House Publishing, 1999), 638.

2. George Herbert, "Love III," *The Country Parson, The Temple*, ed. John N. Wall, Jr. (New York: Paulist Press, 1981), 316.

Chapter 6: Christ to Win Me

1. John Donne, "Holy Sonnet XIV," *The Complete Poems and Selected Prose of John Donne*, ed. Charles M. Coffin (New York: Modern Library, 1952), 252.

2. Francis Pott, translated from Latin hymn, c. 1695, "The Strife Is O'er," *The Presbyterian Hymnal* (Louisville: Westminster/John Knox Press, 1990), 119.

3. Anna Louisa Walker Coghill, "Work, for the Night Is Coming" (1864). http://www.preciouslordtakemyhand.com/christianhymns/workforthenight .html.

4. Dylan Thomas, "The Force That Through the Green Fuse Drives the Flower," *The Poems of Dylan Thomas* (New York: New Directions Publishing, 2003), 90.

5. Samuel John Stone, "The Church's One Foundation" (1866), *The Presbyterian Hymnal* (Louisville: Westminster/John Knox Press, 1990), 442.

6. Thompson, "The Hound of Heaven," 638.

7. Ibid., 642.

8. U. A. Fanthorpe, "Getting It Across," *Selected Poems* (London: Penguin Books, 1986), 72.

9. Anne Lamott, *Grace (Eventually): Thoughts on Faith* (New York: Riverhead Books, 2007), 29.

Chapter 7: Christ to Comfort and Restore Me

1. Thomas Hardy, "In Tenebris," *Collected Poems of Thomas Hardy* (London: Macmillan and Co., 1932), 153.

2. Sir Thomas Wyatt, *The Poetical Works of Sir Thomas Wyatt* (Boston: Little, Brown, 1854), 228.

3. Wendell Berry, "The Slip," *Collected Poems, 1957–1982* (San Francisco: North Point Press, 1985), 224.

4. Cliff Ashby, "A Stranger in This Land," *Oxford Book of Christian Verse* (Oxford: Oxford University Press, 1981), 297.

Chapter 8: Christ Beneath Me

1. William Bryant Logan, *Dirt: The Ecstatic Skin of the Earth* (New York: Riverhead Books, 1995), 15.

2. Ibid., 16.

3. Susan Griffin, *Made from This Earth: An Anthology of Writings by Susan Griffin* (New York: Harper and Row, 1982), 340.

Chapter 9: Christ Above Me

1. Robert Grant, "O Worship the King," 1833.

2. David James Duncan, *God Laughs and Plays: Churchless Sermons in Response to the Preachments of the Fundamentalist Right* (New York: Triad Books, 2007), 208.

3. Nicene Creed.

4. Ibid.

5. Denise Levertov, "Ascension," *The Stream and the Sapphire* (New York: New Directions Publishing, 1997), 83.

Chapter 10: Christ in Quiet

1. Thelma Hall, *Too Deep for Words: Rediscovering* Lectio Divina (Mahwah, NJ: Paulist Press, 1988), 7.

2. Eliot, "Burnt Norton," *Four Quartets*, 15–16.

3. Ibid., 19.

4. Herman Melville, *Moby-Dick*, ed. Andrew Delbanco (New York: Penguin, 2002), 362.

5. Albert Pais, *Subtle Is the Lord: The Science and the Life of Albert Einstein* (New York: Oxford University Press, 1983).

6. BBC News offers one report on this phenomenon: http://news.bbc .co.uk/2/hi/health/342256.stm.

7. T. S. Eliot, "East Coker," *Four Quartets* (New York: Harcourt, Brace, Jovanovich, 1943), 26.

8. Mary Oliver, "When I Am Among the Trees," *Thirst* (Boston: Beacon Press, 2006), 4.

Chapter 12: Christ in Hearts of All That Love Me

1. Virginia Woolf, *To the Lighthouse* (New York: Harcourt, Brace & Co., 1927, 1955), 192.

2. Wendell Berry, "Fidelity," *Fidelity* (New York: Pantheon Books, 1992), 113.

3. C. S. Lewis, *The Four Loves* (New York: Harcourt, Brace, Jovanovich, 1971).

Chapter 13: Christ in Mouth of Friend and Stranger

1. Old Sarum Primer, 1514. Prayer reproduced on the pillars of the old Coventry Cathedral, Coventry, England.

Marilyn Chandler McEntyre (PhD, Princeton University) is a professor of English at Westmont College in Santa Barbara, California. She writes broadly across a number of interest areas, including American literature, spirituality and devotion, medical themes, and poetry. A former columnist for *Christianity Today*, McEntyre is the author or editor of ten books.